THE GIRL BEHIND THE CAPE

How I Found My Depth, Voice and Value from within

NATALIE FALICZ

Dedicated to the deepest parts of you - the place inside of you where the freedom to be all of you exists.

"If you suffer it is because of you,

If you feel blissful it is because of you.

Nobody else is responsible – only you and you alone.

You are your hell, and you are your heaven, too."

Osho

Table of Contents

Introduction

The *Girl Behind the Cape* is designed to go beyond the surface of who you are. It is designed to speak to the internal part of you that houses your soul. By expressing openly and honestly the journey of my life and the many areas in it, it is my wish to take you deep into this heart of mine and to give you full access to what goes on inside of me. Ultimately, I would love for you to find reassurance and take comfort in knowing YOU ARE NOT ALONE.

No matter who we are or what we look like, we all have inside of us an amazing amount of depth, a voice and a story that is unique to us. So often we are being conditioned to turn away from everything that feels true to our hearts. Perhaps we are too afraid to acknowledge that depth, put volume to our voice, and write our own story. Many of us take comfort in the exterior suits we armour ourselves in—the cape we hide behind to shield us from pain, suffering and acknowledging who we were born to be.

Whether it be the corporate uniform we put on for the work week, the business suit we wear onto a plane, the gym wear for the mummy drop-off, the high viz for the tradie day or the all-black outfit for the salon day, we all have capes we disguise our deeper self behind. It's there, underneath our exterior, we will find the truth of who we really are and what we really stand for. If only we grew up learning that this is the ultimate place to live from.

It was only when I began my journey as a hairdresser, when I was given the physical task of placing a cape around my clients' necks, that I began to see the significance of the phrase that 'what's happening on the inside isn't always a true reflection of what you see on the outside'.

Over the past 20 years, I have been given the opportunity to listen to many people use their voice to open up and speak their truth. It's here in this powerful process where I got to witness real beauty, which is always internal and radiates outwards. There is truly nothing more beautiful and profound than watching a person be courageous enough to speak their truth and honour where they are in life and do it all, without agenda. These are the voices that ignite healing and make a real difference in the world and the people in it.

Behind everyone façade, (in my circumstance, cape) we may all be different souls with different soul lessons, but we are all living a human life having a human experience. A lot of our issues fall under the same categories, i.e.: love, grief, loss, suffering, happiness, health, family, self-discovery, to name a few. Two decades of listening has shown me that so many of us are going through the same things, at the same time. So many people feel so alone and isolated in their feelings and where they are in life—myself included—but I have learnt (as you will read in this very book) that's simply not the case.

Let me show you.

****

At 8 years old, I became conscious of my emotions. It was in those early days that I began to journal in diaries and hide them away where no one would find them. Writing was my way of using my voice and expressing my true heart's emotions. No matter what, the pages in my books always accepted my thoughts, my feelings and my perspective. When I put pencil to paper, I felt an instant sense of release. Whatever life looked like on the outside, it was a different feeling for me on the inside. In a lot of ways, writing felt like a safe way to communicate my feelings and not upsetting anyone in the process. No matter what, I could write it down and it would officially be released into a place where the subject matter could properly be seen for what it was, and not for what it was not.

My journals were full of Natalie. In many ways, writing was a way of discovering who I was — it was a way of connecting to myself. I believe I was born with enormous amounts of passion. I had drive, motivation and an abundance of joy. I may have been young, but I remember my spirit was full and overflowing with unconditional love for life and, most importantly, for me. I liked the temporary feeling of finding out who I was and connection with the inner me. It was not until I stopped writing, closed the pages, and returned outside to my life, that I became the Natalie that I *needed* to be. The challenge for me was learning how to stay connected to my spirit, my true self, all while existing in a world where high self-worth, passion for life, joy and not suffering were seen as unrelatable and formidable sensations.

For a short time, I was a full tank, overflowing with light. I was more than happy to share my light and give it to those that needed it. In fact, I was quick to learn that the more I gave, the less I would shine, and when I shine less, I earn more love and acceptance and fit into the environment in which I was placed. Learning how to control my light was an advantageous strategy I developed very early on. It pacified emotional situations I couldn't quite understand. I soon learned that if I keep giving, play small and be of service, I would eventually find my place in my one and only environment.

Without even knowing it back then, this was the beginning of saying goodbye to my self-worth. It was the beginning of the disconnection that separated me from the child I was within. It was the beginning of saying goodbye to what I have taken 36 years to regain and connect back to. The me I left behind because I chose to hand myself over to a name, a hierarchy that only served to breed more of who they were and less of something unfamiliar.

Writing was the way my soul kept me from falling into the dark. Writing was my soul trying to keep me conscious of what I was living in. Writing was a safe way of expressing myself without upsetting anyone in the process. What I was unaware of back then was that there was something special I kept hidden within these books, something that was unique to me and gifted to me at birth, something that I now would never trade; that special gift was my voice—my one essential tool that held me hostage to my circumstance because I believed I didn't have a right to use it. The more I wrote, the more I felt alive; it connected me to a sense of self-confidence I couldn't manage to grasp outside of the pages. Writing was my voice, and it was a safe way to use it. The feeling was warm, it felt safe, and it was freeing. I desperately wanted to take this feeling of alignment into my everyday life, but the more I felt connected, centred, and grounded within myself, the heavier life would be for me when I stopped writing, shut the pages of my book and returned outside into human conditioned life.

The true, deep and passionate Natalie was never going to be truly accepted outside of the pages of her books. I choose to let go of what was not fully accepted and chose to conform to what I needed to do and be in order to earn love—a choice that I would never make again. I stopped writing personally for many years and instead chose to take advantage of places that provided opportunities to do so, like my school's public speaking competitions and debate teams. English became my favourite subject as it gave me many opportunities to write and write to my heart's content. Writing at school gave me great joy; it was only ever really filling a shallow void inside of me as writing about personal feelings and deep emotions was what my heart desired most.

Fast-forward a decade later, I left school and became a fulltime hairdresser. It was during this experience where I was given the largest opportunity to witness the many different types of feelings and emotions that so many people go through. It was the perfect platform to soak up, study and absorbed human behaviour. The simple task of placing a cape around someone's neck gave me the opportunity to become the girl behind the cape—the one not only performing a beauty service but providing them a place of compassion and a place to go deep if they needed it. Listening to them expressing themselves over a 45-minute cut or a two-hour colour service gave me the opportunity to sit back and take in the many stories people had inside themselves. Whether it was in the present, in the past or worrying about the future, there was always something somebody was going through or something that they wanted to talk about and get off their chest. In a way, I felt like I was their journal; I was the blank piece of paper and I handed them the pen by allowing them to feel comfortable enough to open up, and when they did, they began to write. Not physically with a pen, but vocally with their voice.

This whole process made me realise that there are many people who keep parts of themselves suppressed, even hidden, just like I did when I was little. I realised that so many people chose to sacrifice their true selves in order to be loved or fit into a conditioned environment. In many ways, I was honoured that people chose to open up to me, that they felt safe and that they saw that I was someone that would understand. To this day, I value authenticity and seeing people open up and express their authentic selves has been truly inspiring to me. Despite being told that I'm too sensitive for most of my life, I have learnt that I am an empath, and I am proud of it. It has given me the ability to connect with people on a deeper level and, in most cases, I feel like I have been on the ride with them.

Over time, I have heard and felt deeply people's anguish and pain, but also their passions and desires and their want for more or a way out but just not knowing how or having the self-belief to go through with it. I was more than happy to provide a place where people felt heard and seen for who they were. I wanted them to feel as good on the inside as they left looking great on the outside. **Beauty for me is an internal job and an outside reflection**.

I'm no doctor or psychologist. I'm also not someone that believes I have the right to hand out my version of what's right and wrong. I never had the answers, as I don't believe anyone has another person's answers for them. Answers are an internal, individual, and personal conclusion. What's more, I don't want to give anyone the feeling that I am more superior, or that I know better than the person that's sitting in the chair in front of me because I most definitely am not. My approach was more about making them see that they already had the answers within themselves.

In my early days, I just took it all in, listening and observing, unless asked otherwise. As time went on, there was the continual thought of "if only these people knew that they are not alone, that so many others feel the same way". Over twenty years of hairdressing, the topics began to fall under the same categories—relationships, marriage, health, travel, careers, kids, love, pregnancies, schooling and, by far one of the most talked about, family.

Over time, the salon became a place of productive communication. An appointment with me meant that the magazines were never touched, and the phone was never checked. It was a place of soul-deep vocal journaling. Placing the cape around their necks and having them face-to-face with a mirror can be extremely confronting, especially if they are willing to look within. No matter who they were or what they looked like, I saw how the experience brought out vulnerability in each individual. It was my time to exercise extreme compassion and understanding.

I, too, know very well what it's like to be the girl sitting down behind the cape, feeling exposed and vulnerable to either my physical appearance or emotional thoughts staring right in front of me. Being the girl standing behind the cape gave me the opportunity to experience seeing self-worth issues peak.

Still, to this day, it's the first thing I want to help get rid of. The pain I saw in them, I saw in me. I didn't want my clients or anyone I knew to feel unworthy in any way. That is too much for me to bear; seeing them suffer was like opening up my wounds of suffering with them. With their consent, I wanted them to hear my stories so they wouldn't feel so alone in theirs, and perhaps they could use some of my resources to help them heal.

I knew my voice had wisdom and although I didn't believe in myself a lot growing up, I believed in the truthfulness of my heart and intentions. This was to be of service to those that needed it and not take advantage of it. (Spoiler alert: there was a path I had to discover to get to that very place that will be openly spoken about in the chapters ahead).

Truth be told, it's later on in my hairdressing career that I can say my clients have given me tremendous inspiration, love and support through finding their own voices. I feel like the shoe may be on the other foot or perhaps that we equally share the shoes. Either way, behind the cape is a beautiful balance of being seen and heard.

My appointments became about internal worth, exposing self-love, seeing one's individuality and thriving in it. A time of deeply expressing your inner self not your shallow egoic self (we all have one). In fact, now, all the relationships in my life operate from that deep soul-nurturing place.

It never ceases to amaze me how, by opening your heart and speaking from an authentic space, using your voice to express your feelings and vulnerable emotions, stripping back all the layers of humanness and exposing your true self can be the one voice, the one moment, that sparks a light in someone else's darkness. When someone can see some form of light, they don't feel so alone and in the dark. The only way we can truly be of soul-nurturing service is if we are honest, vulnerable and real.

We must be honest with ourselves and our intentions and who we are so we can communicate the truth. We must be courageous enough to be vulnerable and speak up about the non-mainstream way we may be feeling, and real enough to live by the words we speak. It isn't enough to just say them, we have to add weight to the words by being the example. Everyone has felt when someone is "talking the talk" but is empty on the inside, like there is no depth to what they are saying and that they're just quoting the majority. We are not having a majority human experience; we are having an individual human experience.

So, it's here in the pages of this book where I express my individual human experience. This book is based on one journal I have chosen not to hide. Instead, I have written openly and from a place of deep passion. Writing this book has been an enduring marathon, running back to regain the passionate soul-felt, driven young girl that loved to live in light. This book made me realise how much of myself I gave up, how much of myself I lost to low self-esteem. On the other hand, it has also made me realise how resilient I am, how strong I have become and how much I can whether and never truly be knocked down. I'm still here; my soul and spirt are still alive and well and my wish is for you to feel the same.

Our souls can only die if we let them; our spirits diminish if we allow it. Our physical bodies play a small part in who we really are. By giving up who I was and living in the shadows or the dark, I found enough light to get me back to the girl I left behind.

It is one of my many intentions that, while reading the pages of this book, you feel supported, seen and loved unconditionally, for who you really are—the internal you, the only you. It is my wish that, every time you open this book, you imagine that I am standing behind you, about to wrap a cape around you, ready for an internal service of love and support. I hope my opening up and sharing my stories and life experiences gives you comfort and support throughout yours. I pray that my words extract the feeling of isolation from within you and replaces the negative internal dialogue of "nobody understands me, nobody is going through this but me, and there must be something wrong with me" with words of comfort and understanding and relatability letting you know that I have felt the same way and, not only me, but 20 years' worth of outstanding clients. I don't claim this book to be "the truth", but it's *my* truth that feels honest, real, and right to me and the human life I have to date experienced.

If you're reading this and you find that it's not for you, I ask that you perhaps pass it to someone who is struggling in these areas. It may just be the few or 80,000 words their soul may be asking to receive. I also invite you to look at what might trigger you as our triggers are the absolute best place to begin our personal healing journey.

I have divided this book into seven parts. Each part represents a significant time in my life. I begin the book with being birthed into this world and end with where I am today. Within each part, I have segregated each section into chapters. One of the reasons I have chosen to structure my book like this is to evoke communication on the matters I discuss. I have highlighted many different areas in life where you can not only go deep into your own personal journey but use the name and titles to perhaps be a guide in showing someone else how you feel and what you may have been trying to say. I have even been a little creative and used some imaginative analogies and metaphors to explain some common scenarios in some not-so-common ways.

Simply put, this book may even help you to know that I am a normal, common everyday gal; in fact, I really hope it does. My aim is to be relatable which brings comfort and ease; that feeling in itself creates togetherness. I don't want to be separate from you and I don't want you to feel separate from me. Disconnect is cold and isolating—the complete and polar opposite of what I want my book to achieve. I hope you find warmth, connection and comfort within all my pages. This book is not just for girls—it's as much for the men as it is for women. In fact, I have a section dedicated specifically for men. The issues I discuss throughout this book are for humans—gender is irrelevant.

I believe in all my heart that, not only this book, but every book, has a frequency and energy of its own. Depending on where you are in your own personal journey determines what level that frequency is running and what it's willing to accept.

If it's your time, I know my book will find you. I promise you, you're not alone.

Now, take a seat and let me get you caped up.

Love, Natalie.

Natalie
23rd March 1984

Part 1
Identity

"If you don't go within, you go without."

Neale Donald Walsch

From as far back as I can remember, the ability to feel deeply has been a part of who I am. Although growing up I didn't understand a lot of what I felt, it certainly didn't stop me from feeling it. Navigating my way through life and operating from the inside out brought with it many challenges. So, as a form of survival, I learnt to do the opposite and adopt certain ways to exist outside of who I was—a choice I would never make today. At that time in my life, this proved to be a much easier way of being accepted and loved.

Unfortunately, giving away the depth of who I am and choosing to leave my value and my worth to be depicted by people around me not only gave my power and self-worth away, but it eradicated all forms of my true, real, internal identity. When you don't connect to the core of who you are on the inside, you cease to exist and operate by your external, human form, which merely only plays a small part. Being seen for my depth, my passion, my heart has been all I have truly ever wanted in life. However, it wasn't until I woke up and listened to life and the many paths it has taken me, I realised that I am responsible for finding my way back to me. If I want to be seen for more than what I present externally, then I have to find my way back to my true identity and be courageous enough to live from it.

She Has Blonde Hair and Blue Eyes and Answers To The Name of Natalie

Of course, I don't remember what it feels like to be born; I can't remember choosing my birth family or choosing my Earth suit (my human body). While, on a soul level, I believe I chose this, on a human level, I'm on a constant path of learning and discovering, trying to find ways to return to me—the me that I lost or perhaps never found. I was born into a family of five, myself being the eldest. I never chose my blonde hair, blue eyes, size or tall physique. Little did I know, this appearance would feel like a curse and a cross to bear in this lifetime. Perhaps it is my biggest journey to discover how to wear it and how to exist in it.

I do recall a time when I was a little girl where appearance had no value to me. I was able to dance joyfully and skip around feeling happy and free. If I was happy, I would shout it out, dance it out, strike a pose, to get it out. Joy was joy. Looking back now, it seemed like such a short time. When did life get so complicated? *When did all that joy get replaced with such seriousness? It felt like one day I was seven years old and the next morning I was seventeen. Certainly, we all need to grow and evolve, but why does it have to start so young for some of us?*

Was I born with a voice? Well, of course, I was; I was one of the fortunate ones that was blessed being able to speak. I believed I used it to talk, ask for things, say "please" and "thank you", cry and get upset—all those typical things. What I really look back and question are: When did I lose my voice? When did I lose the voice that was gifted to me at birth? Did I ever discover that I had one or that I was allowed to have one?

For the first decade of my life, I got away with using what I call my generic voice. That seemed to be fine and very well-accepted in my household. I had no opinions and, like I said, I pretty much obeyed what I was told to do. It gave me joy and pleasure in doing so. I simply kept doing what felt right and what I was guided to do. This was the beginning of conditioning, people-pleasing, and the start of no self-value. This first stage in my life is what I call no voice recognition.

Give me an S. Give me an E. Give me an S, E, L, F, B, E, T, R, A, Y, A, L. What does that spell? Self-betrayal!

Oh, if I only stayed this way, like a perfect, quiet little princess, my whole life would look completely different. If I stayed this way, I would have to rename my life the story of self-sabotage and self-betrayal. Even in writing this, I feel as though I didn't give much credit to the first ten years of my life; this was the narrative I was living in. Well, how much control do you think you have in your life when you are that young, how identified are you with your inner self, your character, your personality your likes and dislikes. You're still discovering how to walk, how to talk, how to be a member of a school society—your first look into socialising and friendships. I do, however, believe some people are much more connected within themselves than others from a young age. Unfortunately, I was not one of them.

I guess I could describe my early years like a grocery bag—I was needed to carry items and take them in. However, the actual bag never realises what's inside. Its purpose is to just take things on and carry the load. What I never realised was that, for the first ten years of my life, I was already being conditioned into what was expected of me and shown how to feed others complacency. I was born to give myself up to keep the family's matriarchal system alive. Damn my soul for wanting more. Damn my soul for knowing that I'm worth more than that.

For the first decade of my life, I didn't even know what a soul was. I had absolutely no idea about intuition and what self-belief was. Hierarchy was enforced and seen as of utmost importance, and I certainly was not going to disobey that. There were people in authority over me and that meant I was below them, and if that was the case, speaking my truth and using my voice was considered disrespectful.

The next ten years were to be a reflection of what I had learnt and put into practise. In other words, I just kept quiet and took it all on. Hello, anxiety. Hello, panic attacks. Hello, that sick feeling like you've been punched in the stomach repeatedly. How are you? We are apparently going to be quite closely aquatinted for the next decade. All because I don't know any better. I have no identity, don't use my voice or trust gut feelings, and haven't placed any value on myself. We are officially going to take over and have a huge part to play in my emotional wellbeing, resulting in even more consequences for you to deal with later on in life—the price I was to pay for not finding or knowing my worth. I was a little girl who had no internal dialogue.

Please Don't Call Me a Barbie, It's Actually Really Mean

What is identity? Am I allowed to be a person that has feelings? What is the difference between feelings and emotions? Am I allowed to express myself the way other people show me they do? I was a walking, talking human doll or troll, witch or scrub whatever you would like to call me. I certainly wouldn't know or speak up about it. I just go with doll because I was always bullied and spoken down to because, apparently, I looked like a barbie. Gosh, I disliked barbies; I refused to play with them. To me, they represented segregation and separation from any form of friendship I was so desperately wanting to have. One day, I walked into class and noticed that someone left a barbie doll mirror on my desk. I picked it up and looked straight into it; everyone laughed. It felt like everyone took such great pleasure in seeing me upset and alone.

Yes, I had long, blonde hair. It was natural, and I was born that way. To be truly honest, I loved the colour then, and I love it now. Even though I tint it, it is still the colour of my choice. Having been called a princess at home added to me feeling segregated by my family. It sounds nice and sweet, and perhaps it was nice and sweet, but it gave me a conditioned image that I felt I had to live up to. It enabled the 'good girl' façade that was being formed around me. It still makes me squirm to this day.

I don't like some of the things a traditional princess represents—keep quiet, smile, do what is required of you. It seems like princesses are used to giving an artificial representation of a family. They represent no voice and no opinions, just an image. They are to uphold the image that is the complete opposite of what is actually going on inside. I believe that there is so much more to them than what we see and what they show us. Being put on a pedestal because I did everything they wanted and spent my days pleasing them felt inauthentic and superficial. You should never put anyone on a pedestal. The only way off is down, and some people take great pleasure in watching you fall.

The Empty Recipe That Fed Their Hunger

I was always pleasant to everyone. I soon learnt that if I do what I know best—be polite, don't speak, listen to other people's issues, show them that I understand and take on their problems—then there I had it, I became an instant friend and a perfect daughter. I was shown love and acceptance. I would build them up and keep myself down. I acted small (well, I can say that now because I'm an adult and I can see my mistake). I wasn't in touch with me; I didn't even know who 'me" was. It was no one's fault but my own.

I grew up with common sense, values and morals. I grew up knowing how I needed to behave and what I need to do to earn conditional love. If only I knew then what I know now. "You can't put an old head on young shoulders". Well, what if you can? What if you knew exactly how things would play out and they did exactly that? What if your intuition was being supressed because others saw your potential, saw your light, but you hadn't recognised it yet within yourself?

As a young girl, I didn't know how to trust my feelings. I didn't know my feelings were even a thing. What I knew was that feelings were what other people had. What other people were entitled to. When I was exposed to seeing others have them, I always felt a huge obligation to rush in and save them, to help them not feel pain sorrow, or sadness. When they felt better, and I took on their problem (took their problem away from them and replaced it with loving words of wisdom and sincerity), I was befriended, free to go on my way and allowed the right to freedom.

Freedom to me means that no one wants anything from me, whatever I give is enough. It means that I'm allowed to laugh, smile and make my own choices. Freedom is when my soul and my human body align and find peace. Freedom is what I wish for all the people I love to feel daily. It's within all of us, if we have the courage to find it and honour it authentically. Freedom also means that no one owns the right to my happiness. Back then, this is what my recipe looked like:

> Making others happy = Good Girl = Acceptance = Friendships = Love = Happiness = Worth = Value.

As you can see, I was not at all connected with myself or my voice. It wasn't until my late primary, early high school, days that my so-called recipe started to fall short. Having not established an identity within myself, one was therefore created for me.

That's how life works, right? Until you become witness to the choices you make and cast your eyes on the things you see and don't want to see, life will continue giving you exactly what you project. I was not in the driver's seat of my own life and, as I got older, my motor needed oil. It needed servicing and it needed to be refilled in order to keep working. Did I refuel it? No! That would mean putting my needs ahead of others'. That didn't feel comfortable at all to me. Did I break down? Well, that's a matter of opinion.

A View From the Outside is Just a View; Until You Come Inside and See What it's Like, You Will Never See the Real Picture

From the outside looking in, it looked like the typical Natalie was blessed and had it all. Natalie can't relate to me. She can't relate to any of my problems. Let's make her feel extremely outcast and alone just like we feel for looking and feeling the way we do. What would she know about dieting? I was always judged for my size. However, being tall and skinny did not buy me any friends. I can remember eating ice-cream and bread before bed just to put weight on so I would be accepted. Oh, what a problem to have.

My question to that would be: Why? I love the taste! Ok, I get that. But why would you want to subject yourself to doing something so artificial and inauthentic just to please someone and be accepted? Every spoon of ice-cream I consumed felt like I was digging a cold scoop of self-worth out and swallowing a mouthful of self-betrayal. I didn't resemble relatability or what looked like their idea of it.

I come from a household where money was an uncertainty; frivolous spending was not an option. Money was something you worked hard, long hours for. The advantage to that is that you become very savvy very quickly, especially with what to cook and how to dress. To this day, I class myself as a savvy dresser. I once won a Melbourne Cup Fashions on the Field with a dress that cost $14.95. I still feel extremely proud of that accomplishment. It still makes me laugh when I think of this one group of women that came up to me and asked me where I got my dress from. When I told them where I got it and how much it cost, they paused and half-smiled in shock. It still makes me laugh today. Still, though, not as much as 20 years ago when I was getting clothes pulled off of me because I was seen as looking better than someone else.

One night, the phone rang. It was one of the girls from school inviting me to a party. I was delighted to even be asked. Not only was I invited to the party, but I was also told I could get ready with the rest of the girls. I was overjoyed and felt so happy to be included. At the end of the phone call, one of the girls informed me that they only wanted to invite me because they wanted the boys to come. I went from feeling elated to feeling incredibly low. Once again, I was just a pawn in someone else's game, used once more for representation and artificial purposes, not for what was on the inside and who I actually was.

They all laughed, being quite passive and degrading in their delivery, making sure that this was the *only* reason I was needed and invited. I felt small and used. At that moment, they wanted to use my identity for their personal gain. Me being me (the version of me 20 years ago) went along with it as I didn't want to disappoint anyone. It's ok for me to take a hit, suppress it and not speak about it. I didn't want to make anyone unhappy, just myself.

On the day of the party, we all got dressed together. We all brought a bag of clothes so we could swap and see if we wanted to wear or borrow something of each other's—a game I was always happy to play but not all the players were happy to participate. As soon as nothing fit them, they instantly started insulting my clothes and throwing around insults like "Don't you eat anything? Are these children's clothes? They look like they're from the Op shop." I quickly learnt to only bring hats, scarfs, shoes, makeup and jewellery. One size fits all. Those items mean I can avoid being called anorexic and bulimic. I can avoid being ostracized in a group of girls.

That night, I remember wearing a beautiful, flowery dress, topped off with some flats and a lovely cut denim jacket. I secretly loved that denim jacket and I remember feeling pretty in it. We all left and walked to the party as it was just down the street. While I was walking, I felt happy, no matter what had transpired. Whatever ulterior motives existed; I was walking with a group of girls to a party I was invited to.

While enjoying that moment, I remember jumping and twirling along the footpath, swinging my arms wide open, wearing a great smile on my face. As I slowed down, I could see a group of girls at the back. One of them was walking at a very fast pace, directly towards me. She did not stop or even slow down her rigorous pace. Before I knew it, I was flung right back around again, only this time, having my jacket torn right off me, leaving me knees-first on the floor, jacketless.

She took my jacket, stared me in the eyes and said, "You don't need this." Everyone remained quiet as I continued at a slow, solemn pace till we arrived at the party. Stupid me! Why did I have to show happiness? Why did I show a moment of freedom, skipping and swinging around, enjoying myself? That's not going to win me any friends. No one wants to see me *that* happy. I should have known better. I had a moment of weakness. I actually don't remember anything after that point. There was nothing worth remembering when you keep yourself quiet and act small, which is most likely exactly what happened and why I have no recollection of the rest of that night. This is absolutely not an ideal way to live life. This became my learned behaviour around girls, soon to become my adopted behaviour around females in general.

I tried placing myself in environments where image was highly considered—dance classes, gymnastics, ballet—but all I found was that it didn't feel right to me. It didn't align with me, internally. These environments did not represent who I was on the inside. It only made me feel more uncomfortable in my own skin. How I felt on the inside never seemed to match the environment I found myself existing in.

Acquaintance Vs Friendship—There's a Big Difference

Slowly, as time progressed into high school, I became affiliated with the word "acquaintance"—a person one knows slightly, but who is not a close friend. There were a lot of acquaintance relationships surrounding me when it came to females; they all seemed shallow and self-serving, competitive and jealous. It wasn't until I met my one true authentic relationship in a friend, Sam, that everything began to shift. He was a boy, yes, and an amazing, down-to-Earth, kind-hearted, sincere, black-and-white, non-jealous, non-manipulative, tons of fun, honest, kind of person. Not to mention he was the first person that wanted nothing from me. Sam just seemed to like me for me.

After experiencing such an authentic friendship, I started feeling free and happy. I began expressing myself, my thoughts and my views more and more. Sam held space for me. He gave me an opportunity to have a voice. He didn't care what size I was and how I looked; that was all irrelevant. I guess he just liked *something* about me. I know what you may be thinking, the most human common-sense answer is, "Nat, he fancied you." Well, I can tell you wholeheartedly that that was totally not true! The best thing about it was that it was a completely platonic relationship—both ways. I will forever be grateful to Sam for seeing past my external appearances and giving me a chance. After what felt like a sea of shallow cold water, I was now swimming in what felt like a deep, warm, genuine ocean. I have finally had a taste of a real friendship.

Sam and I never let each other down because we were completely independent of one another and, most of all, never placed expectations on one another. That is the fastest way to end any relationship. Another highlight was that we didn't owe each other anything. We were there for each other when I started showing interest in guys and I was there when he was interested in girls. We supported each other with our little crushes and even through my not-so-good relationship choices. No matter what, he stood by me.

Sam became school captain as many others, including teachers, saw the value he brings into everyone's life. How was I so fortunate to end up with a friend like this? Sam valued me for who I was. He allowed me to find me, and to express it. I never felt like a fragile princess or like my appearance mattered to him in the slightest. I am forever grateful to him. What a beautiful human being.

So, This Is What That Feeling Feels Like

Looking back, now I can see that this was my first real awakening to Natalie. I had access to a voice—my voice. Feeling gradually more confident to use it, I had now found myself in situations where others wanted to see what all the fuss was about. Other females had begun giving me a chance as they wanted a slice of the happiness pie they so shrewdly witnessed from a distance. I was starting to be seen as more than what I looked like. Some people liked what they saw, others wanted to give it a go while some others, well, just couldn't. That's fine, of course. I mean, I'm not everyone's cup of tea. As time went on, I realised that more male friendships were coming into my life—some platonic and some not. More male friendships meant more simplicity, no comparison, no judgement. They wanted to hear what I had to say. This was fun, easy and supportive, and how friendships can be.

While I was enjoying my days of happiness and freedom, some other girls (always bloody girls) were not enjoying watching this new form of attention flowing my way. I didn't see it as attention. Hell, I disliked attention. Back to my recipe book:

Attention = Jealousy = Bulling = Saying all these nasty words to push me down off that pedestal you see me being put on.

Don't you girls know that I already feel small and inadequate inside and experiencing friendships brings me joy and gives me hope? They help give people a different perception of me than the one you are trying to create.

Two Words I Wish I Could Remove From Language

"Jealousy". I even dislike using the word "hate", but I really and truly do hate the word and association to jealousy. I would go as far as saying jealousy is a condition—a condition people trap themselves in, a condition that feeds the ego to its fullest. "Comparison" comes in a close second. I'm mad that I even have the words in my book, but for me to expose my experience with these words, it's necessary.

What I have learnt in recent years is that whatever makes you squirm in your seat and feel uncomfortable is what you need to look at working on the most within yourself. That's where I have spent a lot of time digging deep. This is where a lot of my lessons come from. My goal is to be able to look, write and talk about them without being triggered. I'm nearly there. They are my areas of growth and I do see myself, in the future, using them as allies. Looking back, I see that those two words caused me a lot of pain and grief. They made me realise that these were the lessons, on a soul level, that I signed up for and has put me exactly where I need to be right now, here, writing this book and explaining what it's like being on the receiving end of it. I hope to shed light and compassion on the issue. To this day, it has not defined me but made me stronger and wiser.

So, why, you ask, are these trigger words form me? Let's look at the meaning of "Jealousy"—unhappy or resentful because you feel that someone is your rival or is better or luckier than you. See, that is all yucky stuff. It's horrible and it's the complete opposite of who I am or anything I represent. Anyone that is in a truly healthy headspace does not accept this as a normal response. I have never been able to relate to jealousy. Gosh, it makes me angry. "...because you *feel* that someone is better or luckier than you". Notice the word "feel". In other words, it's not real; it's just an egoic feeling.

If something feels grey, unhappy, unpleasant, then that is not your higher self speaking. That is what I call running on a low vibration. This vibration is driving your pain body and allowing your ego to take full control. As Melissa Ambrosini would call it, "your mean girl" or mean boy—your inner critic. Mean girls or mean boys are always trying to take control of our consciousness. It is up to us to be aware of it and not let them take control of our mind, choices and wellbeing. When you choose jealousy, you are absolutely allowing them full control. Your true, authentic self that is 100% a part of you, would most likely turn jealousy into admiration, which is so much better, kinder, and smarter.

Jealousy is an illusion of not feeling like you have enough or are enough. Although you have seen that I have felt not enough within myself, I never turned to jealousy or resentment as a justification for my feelings. One of the worst side effects of this condition (and to me, jealousy is an unhealthy condition) is that those that choose to adopt the feeling can become unaware they are even bathing in it. Jealousy is a fast pass to unconsciousness and an even quicker way to fall deep into unhappiness.

As you can see, there is nothing pleasant and uplifting in this situation. This unpleasantness has followed me around for decades. I have never once seen it as a confidence booster or a form of flattery—it most definitely was not, especially when I cannot only see, but feel, the resentment behind their eyes. I know I'm not alone in feeling this way. What makes it bearable for me today is that I become aware of it as soon as I see it. I don't personalize it as I see it as a reflection of them and something within them that they have not yet acknowledged and become accountable for within themselves. It has absolutely nothing to do with me. I may be on the receiving end of the condition, but I never choose to become a victim to someone else's nastiness. The moment I do, I have created a problem within myself.

The definition of comparison is "the act of finding out the difference and similarities between two or more people or things". Ok, so this one doesn't seem so bad, right? It's a lot milder. I actually think "comparison" is an essential tool in decision making for, let's say, buying a house or comparing results, determining witch model of car you would like to buy, or a doctor analysing test results. It's an essential part of living. So, let's leave it there, to be used for the greater good; let's not use it for personal justification and measuring value of oneself against another.

There is absolutely no reason to compare yourself with anyone else, good or bad. When you compare yourself to others, you devalue yourself. You are enough just being you. We are all different human beings; we were never born to be the same. Even identical twins have similarities but are different souls. Once we can accept ourselves wholeheartedly for who we are and what we bring into this universe, we will find that there is no need for personal comparison.

There are so many people I admire. I see so many traits, qualities and aspects of their character that I like and look up to. Personally, I believe we need these people in our lives.

Where would we be without the people, places and things we admire, learn and grow from? We all can look at things to aspire to be, especially people we want to learn from. What point in life do we stop using comparison as a tool to measure our own inner worth?

Comparisonitis by Melissa Ambrosini is a must-read. I don't believe that there is anyone that can explain comparison quite like Melissa does. It's incredible.

Part 2
The Working World

"Well, there's one thing they can't order me to do—stop dreaming!"

Cinderella

Entering the working world at a young age has taught me how to mature even more than what I already was. I believe everything absolutely happens for a reason and that each person in our life is placed in our path for a purpose or a lesson, as hard as that lesson may be at times. My journey in the beauty industry by far has been the largest catalyst to exposing me to humanity and all it has inside of it. The simple salon cape had with it great power, it gave me the ability to see through to my client and listen to what their hearts wanted to share. It was here where I began to see that I was not alone in my suffering and in my sorrows.

The salon has taught me not only how to cut and colour hair, but ultimately one of the best skills in life—how to listen. It may have begun rocky, but it has ended solid.

The Next Decade and What I Brought With It

The next decade of my life began at high school and ended when I became a young working woman. Having brought with me all the unacknowledged self-worth and amplified feelings that had not yet been dealt within me. As I had mentioned previously, I had an emotional storm brewing, ready to explode at any point. But did I know that? Did I listen? No! I continued to sail the unconscious sea, pushing myself instead of listening to myself.

It all began for me in Grade 10. While at school, I had taken up work at a local hairdressing salon. I became the 'Tea and Tidy'; I worked Thursday nights after school and all day on Saturdays. It was great experience and my first real job. I instantly enjoyed being of service and getting paid to do so. This was my new little life—I went to school and worked one and a half days a week. I made $79 and I was rich. I could afford to buy anything I wanted and, more importantly, I could start saving. I knew from that $79 a week and that feeling of working that I had begun a new relationship. A relationship that was healthy and that was of equal value. That was my relationship with money.

As weeks turned into months, which quickly turned into nearly a year, I was offered a fulltime apprenticeship. I was never an extremely academic person and had not found my calling in any other field. I knew I loved public speaking, people and being of service. The beauty industry did not sound enticing to me, but it also didn't have any negative connotations either. I remember feeling like it was an opportunity that was presented to me and, because I felt open to it and nothing was holding me back, I decided to take it. There ended my schooling life for me. I finalised school and, the following year, I began my Cert III in Hairdressing.

The Beginning of Maturity

Waking up each day to go to work, not school, was a thrill. I was now a young girl in the working world. It felt amazing and it felt right. I never felt upset about leaving school life behind. It finally felt like I was heading in some sort of 'Natalie' direction. Besides, I already knew everyone at work, and I had an idea of what the job was going to entail. It required long hours on my feet, standing and serving all day, with a great big smile on my face for little pay.

Where I ended up was far from where I began. I don't want to bring out the violin here, but when I first started, it was quite a rough industry to be in. It wasn't loyal, nor was it caring, and it was very self-serving. I remember, when I first started, I was the good girl, people-pleaser. Well, from what you've probably already gathered about me, I brought the no-voice, no-worth Natalie with me into this part of my life. I remember working extremely hard; the hardest I have ever worked in my life. My job entailed meeting and greeting clients, getting them settled with tea, coffee, magazines, sweeping hair, cutting foils, washing hair, cleaning workstations, trollies and so much more. I was responsible for the cleanliness of the entire salon.

The woman there even called me 'Saidy the cleaning lady'. It was completely derogatory and absolutely patronising. I had so much more to offer than what I was being told to do. But hey, we all must start somewhere. I couldn't just be thrown into senior responsibilities; I needed to be a team player and realise that nothing is beneath me, that all jobs big and small are for the greater good. Being a team player was always so important me. I don't know why they treat apprentices like outsiders and non-members, especially when the majority of the time they are the ones keeping the entire team afloat.

Nothing is Insignificant

I lived in a house not far from the salon; it was even within walking distance. That was my first place of residency; my second was this life-changing place known as 'The Basin'—the wash station, otherwise known as the place where your hair is rinsed, and your colour is washed. This hotspot was where I felt I could pitch a tent and take up permeant residency, a place where I spent hours a day on my feet. It's where I credit so much of the strength and resilience I use today. I even call it one of the biggest classrooms I have ever learnt from. Visually, it can be seen simply as a place to wash hair and get an amazing head massage that is much needed. For me, the one standing and washing hair relentlessly all day long, the basin area taught me how to look outside myself and how to push past my own physical pain and adopt a different form of strength. It taught me how to push my mind into being completely present with what I was working on.

When you set your intentions on giving a person the best of your ability, being of service can be the shift that takes away that pain. Suddenly, those achy knees and burning shoulders don't seem so bad when you truly want nothing more than to give your best at any given moment. Compassion is something I looked for in every person, even if it was hard at times. I knew that giving my best all the time would someday result in a rewarding work ethic.

So, in times of what I think is suffering or low vibration, I would always look to create that shift. There was and still is something rewarding when you witness another human being feeling a moment of freedom. Freedom from thought, experiencing peace and feeling completely relaxed. If I can take part in providing that to someone, that makes me feel like I'm fulfilling part of my purpose and therefore brings me joy, like I have accomplished something special.

The basin is one place where people seem to let go and switch off, and I liked being witness to that. In my 20 years of hairdressing, I have honestly only come across one lady who didn't enjoy a head massage (which is totally fine); everyone else seems to love them and look forward to that part. Providing this small but powerful service made me realise how similar we all are. Although, externally, we may have differently shaped heads, hair colours and textures, our internal dialogue is really very similar and the problems we face are not so far apart from one another, despite what we portray.

While shampooing away, clients would open up and pour their hearts out to me. I learnt so much about husbands and businesses, children and schools, illness and getting old, sex and travel. You name it; everything and anything is open for discussion in a salon. It made me mature even more than I already had. I was always happy to be a safe place for people to confide in and confiding in me is what they did. I have always been a girl that treats people the way I would like to be treated. I also believe in karma and not selling people's trust in exchange for inauthentic acknowledgement and a false sense of worth. Yes, they say hairdressers and salons are places for gossip, but they don't have to be. That can all stop with you. As you can see, this is where my integrity started to grow as I made the decision very early on that everything, big or small, that people told me was for me alone. This is a tool I use in my day-to-day life—trust.

So, as you can see, the most tedious and monotonous job taught me some of the biggest and most powerful lessons. It is here where I became the hairdresser that I am today. I want to encourage all aspiring hairdressers to never overlook this place of service. It begins at a spot where you may think is so insignificant but, as we truly know, no person, place or thing is ever insignificant. Everywhere is an opportunity to deliver the best versions of ourselves. I want to offer the best that I can give to everyone and everything and, what I more recently discovered, to myself, too.

There is absolutely no job too small. You can make an impact on people's lives digging a hole and filling it back up again. It's how you choose to do it. The outlook you create is the attitude you develop. That attitude can't be bought; it has to be learnt and developed internally. Your attitude can be defined as your current state of mind while performing a task. Attitude is what will take you from doing to achieving, from being good to being great. Anyone can do, but how many set out to achieve? You can start at the smallest places.

Hunger, Just the Salt Off the Peanut Will Be Fine

Between washing hair, sweeping floors, making coffee, taking appointments, cutting foils, cleaning the salon from top to bottom, refilling shampoo bottles, getting the senior hairdressers their lunch, cleaning brushes, disinfecting combs and so much more, I found it hard to stop, eat and catch my breath. Lunch breaks were not something you took. Well, they were certainly taken out of my wage, but not physically taken in the salon, especially not for a non-smoking apprentice. This was so common back then, but I hope it is not happening now. There were days when I just wanted to pass out from hunger and dizziness; I would work all day and eat on the run, in between my many jobs. To my poor digestive system, I'm so sorry. I still can't believe I never spoke up. I allowed this to happen because I didn't believe I had a right to speak up. I felt like this is what was expected of me, and I didn't want to disappoint. I also didn't want to be replaced.

I would never accept this now but, of course, no-voice Natalie just kept quiet. It's funny admitting this, but I used to take more bathroom breaks than I needed. Quite often, I would take the bathroom keys, walk there, close the door, and just sit. I didn't even have to go. It was the only legitimate reason I could think of to be able to stop for a second. My mind and body were always on the go, there were so many times I felt like I couldn't keep up.

As time went on, my body couldn't function without taking a proper break. I needed to be sitting down while being able to digest my food and getting some fresh air. To this day, I don't mind working my butt off and giving it my all, just as long as I get a chance to catch my breath, eat, drink, regenerate and get back to it. I mean, we don't do our best work when we're running on an empty tank; we're only hurting ourselves and not being of any value to anyone. Now, I would never work for anyone who doesn't appreciate the same values.

As time went on, passing out was inevitable. I didn't listen to what my body was trying to tell me. And if I wasn't going to listen, then my body would have to show me and stop me. It was time I saw a doctor and got some proof that I had pushed myself too far and my body needed nourishment. If I was to continue, I had to find ways to support it and replenish what I was taking out of it.

Finally, I mustered up the courage to inform my then boss about my health issues. I had even shown her proof from my doctor; since I had evidence from a legitimate source, I felt confident enough to confront her about it. Without the evidence, it was just my words, my voice, my feelings, which, back then, meant as much as a bucket of feathers. Once I confronted her—meaning I asked her if it was possible to start taking proper lunch breaks as I was getting them docked from my pay anyway—she replied with a cold, "Ok." For the next few months, that was how I was treated coldly. This was my punishment for speaking up. What did I do when she made me feel small and insignificant? You guessed it; I took it on as if I was responsible for her reaction—another learned behavioural pattern I had picked up from early childhood. I felt responsible for contributing to someone else's unhappiness. Such a massive no-no.

'You are never responsible for anyone's actions or reactions. How they react has nothing to do with you and everything to do with them.'

The words 'she made me feel small and insignificant' are what I use to describe how I felt back then. I was young and unaccountable. But she didn't make me feel that way. I already felt small and insignificant; her choice of words and the way she intended to make me feel would have no effect if I believed in myself in the first place.

Moving On Is Sometimes The Best Thing To Do

As time went on, the situation in the salon did not get any better. I made the adult decision not to continue in that environment as it clearly was not in the best interest for my health and wellbeing. So, I set out to find myself a more supportive working environment. I worked in a few salons but, honestly, finding a place to finish my apprenticeship wasn't easy. The industry wasn't what it perhaps is today. Eventually I found a salon and began working for a lady who smoked like a chimney inside the salon (I believe you could back then). She was voluptuous and full of life She was a fantastic hairdresser, and I became very good at blow-waving, foiling colouring and cutting. I really enjoyed it. I was also attending trade school once a week, which I loved. I had also formed a great group of friends that worked in local salons nearby. We would carpool together and drive an hour north for our day at trade college, which was a lot of fun.

During my time in this particular salon, things began relatively well. I completed enough of my apprenticeship to the point where I started taking my own clients and had people requesting me. It was exciting; there were people out there that actually liked what I was doing and, better yet, they wanted to come back every 6 to 8 weeks to do it again. Not only was it a great feeling to make people feel good about themselves and to see them happy, but to also have developed a skill that I enjoyed, too Things were looking good, perhaps too good.

Connecting With Clients-Humans-Souls

Discovering that I could be of service to someone was such a validating feeling for me, and it still is, especially when it is met with such gratitude and appreciation. To make someone physically feel good was great in itself but making someone feel better internally is beyond words. It lights me up and fuels my purpose. While spending my days working my way through my apprenticeship, I never once stopped and realised that this was the beginning of my soul's calling. Listening to all the stories the clients would share with me would teach me so much about human behaviour. It made me realise that we all go through very similar problems and that we aren't that much different from each other.

It taught me that we as humans place so many expectations on not only ourselves, but others around us. Some things were hard to hear, especially when it came to self-loathing and the lack of love and compassion people had for themselves. To hear it made me feel cold and uncomfortable on the inside, like I had an internal reaction to the words they were using to describe themselves. It was incredibly hard, but a part of my job was to listen to it.

This was the realization that there was a life so much bigger than what goes on in my head. It was the understanding of what goes on outside of me, and outside of my mind. It taught me that, even though I couldn't personally relate to some of them, it didn't mean that I didn't still feel their pain and suffering. I so deeply wanted them to know that they were so much more than the story they were telling themselves and that I truly felt and heard their pain. I just didn't know how to do that back then and I was honestly scared to speak up, thinking that I would hold no credibility being so young. When someone decided to open up like that, I didn't want their bravery to go unacknowledged, so I managed to find something in their narrative to associate with, something that I could visualize and therefore express understanding and compassion towards their emotions.

People have often described their salon appointment as a form of therapy, providing a good few hours to open up and let out the issues and dramas they are currently dealing with. Once finished, they feel a sense of weight lifted off their shoulders. Communication is so powerful; having someone there just to listen with a compassionate heart can do so much.

Having the ability to connect to people is a skill that I love and cherish; and you don't need to be a hairdresser to acquire that skill. I believe in my heart of hearts that if you choose to find that connection with your clients, your friends, your child's teacher, your contractor, all your relationships, big and small, then they will truly work out for your greatest good. When you aim to create that authentic link between one another, the outcome is limitless and advantageous for both of you.

To this day, I have run my business exactly that way; as soon as I meet someone, I look for that connection. Yes, sometimes it can be harder than others, especially when I'm met with ego, but with 20 years of practise, I have learnt to look beyond that. It's generally the ones with the largest egos that need the most love and acceptance in the first place. For anyone else, I have learnt to use my intuition. That was a weak point in the beginning, and each year it grew stronger and stronger. It also grew with my worth. There is absolutely no way I would allow a client into my space to take advantage of me anymore. That would disempower or control me. Rarely, there was the odd occasion that you would come across a client that you just could not connect with. Some stuff is too heavy to carry and having it projected onto you is just not healthy. My current clients and I have a very loving and caring relationship that is of equal value. They mean so much to me and give me so much that I feel I could not even charge them for my services. And it's a completely two-way street. We are really of service to each other. I have learnt not to accept anything less and the minute I made that decision, my clientele tripled, and I have never had to look for business again. Oh, how self-worth, honouring your authentic self and loving yourself pays off, big time. You must try it if you haven't already.

Bullying Comes At All Ages

Before reaching this wonderful place of mutual appreciation I mentioned above, there was one more mountain I had to climb and learn before landing where I did. When it came to my bosses, a similar story was repeating itself—the story that looked exactly like my earlier years when I'd get along with everyone when I played small, had no voice and kept them happy. Instead, this time, there was a difference. As you can see, I had developed skills, took pride and showed joy in my work; it was very hard to hide those things. I was now starting to form bonds with clients; I couldn't exactly disguise the hairdresser and person I was in front of the clients. They got to know and see me for who I was. Many times, I was even requested, and the boss was not liking it. Gosh knows why I was making her so much money. My appointment column was booked out for a month and a half in advance, and I was making my wage and then some. This was not rewarded or promoted; it was met with bullying—an adult acting like a child.

As a young girl, I always suffered with bloating. It was an insecurity of mine, and my boss knew it. One day, I was completing a blow-wave on my boss's hair, as I did weekly for her. For me to complete the blow dry, I needed to stand in front of her to blow-wave her fringe forward. As I moved to do this, my stomach was directly in front of her face. She lifted my top up to my belly button and grabbed my stomach and said, "Look at the size of this, the clients think you're pregnant." It was a memory I will never forget. I felt personally attacked. She hit me right where she knew it would hurt and she had no right to do such a thing. I felt like crying and I felt small, but I said nothing at all out of shock. She laughed as if it was just a small joke; it was to completely knock me off my high vibes and show me who's boss.

Other days, she would grab a product out of my hand when I was finishing up on a client and tell me not to use it, that, "That won't work. Don't be ridiculous, you can't use that on their hair." She was completely condescending. I knew the product would work and look specular, but I just did what I was told and grabbed the product that she had suggested to add to her superiority. On days when she was mad, she would make me pull everything outside of the salon onto the shop's front grass. She had me dragging out all the salon chairs, trollies, overhead dryers, coffee table, reception desk, you name it.

The people in the other shops next to us thought she was mad and lazy as she would just sit there, smoking her cigarette and having her coffee while she watched. During this time, I would vacuum and mop the floor, wipe the windows inside and out and basically clean everything so clean that you could eat your dinner off it. I was Saidy all over again, except this time, I was almost a qualified hairdresser and being punished for being a good one.

Albert Einstein, I Think You're Onto Something

Albert Einstein once said that insanity is doing the same thing over and over and expecting a different result. This is absolutely what was happening here. I was being placed in the exact same situations because I wasn't conscious as to what was going on. Although I can write about it now, years later, back then, I really didn't understand what was going on. Was there a name for it? Was there something I was doing? Yes. I was still quite young and inexperienced, and not wise enough to work it all out. I felt the effects and knew it did not feel right. I wanted a different outcome, but I didn't have the confidence to speak up and do something about it. To some degree, I did all that I knew I could do. That was to leave and find a place that didn't treat people like this. It felt easier to escape and start afresh rather than to try and make it work in a place where I was never heard or appreciated.

That was the Band-Aid fix—to remove myself from that environment. It was, in part, a step in the right direction, but the bigger problem was the issues of self-worth and not speaking up that were repeating themselves over and over until I was able to wake the hell up and see what's in front of me.

In the meantime, the universe had a plan for me to complete my CERT III in hairdressing and land a full-time job. After four years of long, hard work, I had finally earned the right to call my own shots. I was a fully qualified hairdresser and proud I got to the finishing line.

A Change of Scenery Is Just What The Holistic Doctor Ordered

The next few years were all about implementing my new career working title. I began working at different hair salons, hairdressing supply stores and starting up my own mobile hairdressing business. I attended many hair shows and worked for many different hair companies; I really enjoyed experiencing all the different sides of the hairdressing world. Working in the hair and beauty supply stores kept me busy packing orders, stocking shelves, recommending colours and attending up-to-date training with the latest products and techniques. This was a place where I could familiarise myself with the local salon owners from around the suburb.

I enjoyed this job; it was nice to be on this side of the industry. There was one hair supply store that I loved working at the most. This place was owned by two of the most generous and considerate people I've ever met. It was such a pleasure and a relief to be able to work for them as they treated me so well. With this job, I was able to sit down and eat and even take a coffee break. They flew me to the Sydney hair show, all expenses paid. It was so much fun, and I thoroughly enjoyed myself. As I always did, I put in 100% effort, and it was acknowledged and appreciated. They valued my work ethic, and I valued and appreciated how I was being treated. To this day, we still catch up and call each other friends. I felt so humbled by this experience. It was necessary for me to witness what a healthy and supportive working environment looked like.

After experiencing this, I didn't want to return to anything less. In a way I felt like the universe had supported my decision to move on from circumstances that didn't serve me, by gifting me one that truly did.

Throughout It All, There Are Some Things I Know For Sure

Let's get something clear straight up—you know you better than anyone else knows you. If you don't already know and feel it, it just means you may need to reconnect with your inner self so you can access that information. I assure you, it's there. Guidance from professionals is a wonderful resource; I recommend gathering all the information they give you. Ask all the questions—that's what they're there for and that's what they're good at, especially when they have your best interest at heart. Just remember, the more you love you, the more you will love your do.

"The best colour in the whole world is the one that looks good on you."

Coco Chanel

Hairdressers work on external beauty. If you're not happy with who you are on the inside, you will never be truly happy with what see on the outside. Acceptance is a massive player in loving your hair. Accept and then love what you have accepted—that's an award-winning recipe to achieving massive hair goals. I can assure you that what you don't like about your hair, someone else absolutely loves and would be happy to trade up for it. I see it all the time. Most people want what they don't have because they haven't gone through the acceptance process and also haven't been shown how to work with what they have naturally been gifted with.

What most of us haven't realised is that, when you walk into your hair appointment, you already bring with you all the goods you need—you are the incredible foundation. Most importantly, you must have a beautiful relationship with yourself before you can love anything a hairdresser is going to do.

So many girls—and even women—want to look exactly like a Pinterest picture. They have it set in their heads that this is exactly what they want. "If I look like this, then I will feel better. I will look and feel like I want to really feel. Can I just be like the person in the picture?" This is not healthy or authentic; you are so much more than that airbrushed, filtered picture. Don't get me wrong, I love Pinterest and magazines for inspiration and as a form of communication, but not as an end result. Remember, if you were to be photographed like this, with all the bells and whistles, your hair would look like that, too, and perhaps, even better. Similarly, if those people were to be seen in person, their hair wouldn't necessarily look exactly like that. You are more special than any image. You are real, authentic and beautiful; no one has what you have. Don't hide it or cover it up; work with it and you will radiate.

Some of the many amazing qualities I love and admire about my clients is that they don't bring self-criticism with them to their appointments. They also don't need me to make them feel worthy or validated. The ones that did are still searching for that validation. As you are probably aware by now, if you rely on someone to make you feel a certain way, then you will never find that feeling you are looking for. You are giving your power away. And you guessed it—it has to be something you find within yourself. If someone can make you feel something, they can also take it away; if it was yours in the first place, and grown from within you, it will never be truly lost as it was yours to begin with. They're incredible humans, my clients; I have complete admiration for them. They own who they are, and we work with what they have and what makes them special and unique. And believe me, everyone has something.

In many ways, I believe I created this environment. Perhaps, at first, it was even on a subconscious level. I took everything I learnt, liked and disliked, and grew a place where finding your worth and reconnecting with it became a salon experience. For me, it's important to amplify what already exists, instead of recreating, changing and steering away from what makes a person special in the first place.

Mirror, Mirror, On The Wall

"What you resist will persist. What you look at disappears."

Neale Donald Walsch

Can you think of a moment during your week or even your month, when you sat down for over an hour with only your face exposed in front of a mirror? I know there are lots of people that do some form of mirror work, and good on them for doing it. There's no doubting how powerful it can be; you only have to read the amazing Louise L. Hay books to discover how life-transforming it can be.

What about the next time you attend your hair appointment? Use this time to pay close attention to the feelings that arise while you are being caped up. Having a cape clipped around your neck, facing forward, only to realise that you and only you are staring back at you for the next couple of hours, can be a pretty confronting realisation. Just you and the mirror. Notice what comes up. I count myself included in this experience, of course. I've stared into that mirror, taken one look at myself, and chosen to put my feelings on autopilot. Not wanting to acknowledge or face any of what my conscience was trying to make me aware of.

Now, I know better. I use this time wisely, knowing fully well that if I don't acknowledge those uncomfortable feelings, they will keep persisting until I do. Positive thoughts are to be acknowledged, too; it's extremely important that we give credit to ourselves for realising our potential and witnessing our worth. The good has to be rewarded—it must. A personal example of this was when I sat down and saw my skin looking particularly radiant. I made sure I spoke to my internal self by saying, "Natalie, your skin looks really nice today. How awesome does this feel to look into the mirror and be happy to see my skin glowing?" Many other times, though, the first thing I would notice was how tired I was and how many pimples I had.

A regular compliment I have learnt and practised since becoming a mother is, "Natalie, well done for taking the time out for you; for wanting to put time and effort into your human body, you are setting a personal-worth boundary that you are worth putting effort into." Yes, you can laugh, but I do have to talk to myself like this as a way of reminding myself that I am worthy. This is my personal dialogue and the work I have committed to doing in order to shift old programming and become my own worthy identity. I'm constantly doing the work and taking responsibility for what I allow into my space. As you can tell, this is something I have developed over time.

Evidently, I know what it's like to be on both sides of the cape. I know how venerable it can be having only your face and thoughts exposed to you. I also know what it's like being the one standing behind the cape, witnessing all of this going on for someone else.

The Night That Created a Shift

It was only a year ago I was asked to be a speaker at an empowering women's event here in my hometown. This involved me speaking in front of a room of women while also being streamed around the country for those who couldn't physically attend. I was asked to speak my truth. Yes, that's right. Twenty years down the track and I was asked to use my voice to inform women of my views and beliefs on beauty and where it comes from. In my presentation, I included the concept of facing what is in front of you and acknowledging what you see and what you feel. I also spoke about everything I learnt from my 20 years of experience in the beauty industry and everything I have mentioned to you so far in this book. My speech went on for 45 minutes and, despite starting off this life with no voice, I can tell you I found one that night.

I was the first speaker. I was nervous and excited and loved every minute of it. It completely lit me up from the inside. I knew if I could just push past the fear of getting up there, after the first few minutes, I would begin to feel comfortable and my message would come across how it was intended, and that's exactly what happened. I remember seeing all these faces staring at me, listening to me, accepting me with open hearts and open minds, willing to learn and take what information they could to better help themselves.

I couldn't help but hold so much admiration for them. I was in a room where everyone wanted to be accountable for their suffering and learn a new way of dealing with what they were currently going through or working on. This touched me deeply and made me truly see that there are people out there that want to help themselves and just didn't know how. For so many years, I was used to hearing people's stories of suffering and watching them do absolutely nothing or take any form of responsibility for it. It was truly inspiring to be around people that took action for what they wanted, even if they didn't know what that entailed.

Halfway through my presentation, I had given everyone a little exercise to complete. Each person had a pen and paper and was asked to write down three things they loved about themselves—three things that make them unique. Some women found this was easy, which was fantastic, while others took some time to think about it. Ever so sadly, though, there was one woman that couldn't complete the exercise; she told me she couldn't think of anything nice at all to write about herself. She looked at me with this untethered look on her face and uttered those words. It absolutely broke my heart and has stuck with me to this day. I think it was because of the way she said it, like it was normal for her to just naturally and casually declare it. She wasn't attention seeking or trying to draw the conversation her way; she certainly didn't act like a victim nor was she laughing about it. She was just lost for an answer.

From that moment, something changed in me. It's just not good enough for, not only women, but also men and children to exist like this—to struggle to find something within themselves that makes them special, or to find something they love about themselves. We must all hold love for ourselves and access it daily. We must come together, turn on our authenticity, turn on our love, dial down the ego and be kind to ourselves and to one another. If you see something you like in another, say it. Mean it. One kind word can be the shift that someone needs to ignite their self-worth journey.

That night taught me so much; it had been a real turning point in my life. There was a shift that occurred in me. This shift sparked a realisation that there was a side to me that I hadn't accessed completely; that there was more for me to give, and that there was more that I could do. This whole experience lit me up; my insides were screaming at me, "This is where you were meant to end up!" It's like I had my own personal cheerleaders, dancing away cheering me on, confirming I was on the right path. Don't get me wrong, I was nervous as hell and my heart was pounding fiercely. Yes, there's the fear that nobody will listen to me and find value in what I say (that is, ego/false self, mean girl going to town), but I can push past that fear and speak my truth and use my voice to share what I have learnt in hope that it will help others.

"I would rather die trying and fail than not try at all."

What I hope for is to be the reminder of what these individuals have forgotten to see. There is greatness in every single person I see in or out of the salon. When they come to sit down in front of that mirror, get caped up and look straight ahead, it's there that they see the real beauty. Real beauty is deep; it shines through your eyes to your face. When you see yourself for who you really are and accept and love that person wholeheartedly, true beauty has formed—no hairdresser needed.

Part 3
The Mind Muscle

"The waters ahead may not all be smooth sailing, the path of rising change never is. When the seas get choppy know that all of life is working with you, not against you, and that you have everything you need within you to get through any wave, wind, or storm."

Rebecca Campbell

When making the decision to continue to drink from a cocktail of low self-worth, giving from an exhausted emotional tank and not connecting to the truth of who you really are, life soon sends your body several wake-up calls to make you pay attention. There's no use going to the physical gym if you haven't worked on the most important muscle in your body—your mind muscle. Mine was weak and vulnerable; it wasn't until I woke myself up and listened to my internal belief system that I found the right help I so desperately needed.

When you quiet your mind and listen to your heart, it's only then that you will be guided to the right form of help.

Enough Was Enough, I Couldn't Take It Anymore

There comes a point in life when enough is enough, whether you have decided it for yourself, or your mind and body did first. We absolutely must see ourselves as a priority. We must see value in ourselves and as worthy of nurturing our own needs. We are people, too; we need all the love, compassion, and kindness that we so easily give out to others. Have you heard the expression, "Fill up your cup and give from the overflow"? Instead, so many of us continue to give from a half-empty cup and, worse, from a cup that is completely bone-dry. When there is nothing left to give, you're eating into you. You're giving up you in order to keep others alive and well. This was the pattern that was starting to take its toll on my mental wellbeing. What a massive cost on my wellbeing and my identity it was.

For some of us, I know all too well that this is learned behaviour form early years—perhaps, even conditioning from an early age. It's likely that your mother or grandmother was raised in this way, and it was passed down from generation to generation until it was absorbed into your mind that giving up yourself in order to keep others happy was as normal as making your bed in the morning. Can you imagine a world where giving up your happiness and wellbeing in exchange for worth and self-value existed?

For me, this was a prerequisite for being accepted and seen as a good girl and doing the right thing. In my mind, if you did not self-sacrifice, you were classed as "disrespectful" and shunned for not following the elders that gave themselves up to keep matriarchy and a hierarchy system alive. Who do we think we are if we want to break free from this? Who do we think we are if we want to stand on our own two feet and break tradition? Who do we think we are if we listen to ourselves and know that this way is not working for us but against us? All these questions have been thrown at me in my path towards self-worth.

Deep down inside, I knew something was not right. The problem was, however, that I never had the courage to listen to it and believe in myself. Anxiety is a build-up of not listening or going within and dealing with what your gut feelings are trying to tell you. Another way of looking at it is stored-up energy, and not the good kind. Your higher self is trying to get your attention. Are you listening? Was I listening back when I was a young girl, a young adult? No, I didn't know how to, and I wasn't shown how to—until one day, life showed me.

It was late one Sunday afternoon when I started to feel lightheaded, and my heart started to race. Shortly after, my breathing became short and quick. My hands and toes became very cold, and I could hear my own voice echoing back to me when I spoke. I lived with my boyfriend at the time, and he, too, began to notice that I didn't quite look right. He suggested that I took a seat outside for some fresh air, put my head down low and breath between my legs. At that moment, I felt like I was having a complete out-of-body experience. I was at no point in control of myself. I had no tools or the information I know now to help me through it and away from this isolation situation. I remember my boyfriend talking to me and asking me if I was alright, which seemed to just make matters worse. When I was in this uncontrollable state, I just needed to be left alone and not speak to anyone, as every word sounded like someone was screaming directly into my ear. Every time I spoke, my voice screamed out at me and echoed through my mind. It was a really disorienting feeling and one that frightened me. While cold, fresh air and not having to speak seemed to help, it didn't prevent what escalated next. What felt like sharp knives in the centre of my chest was the beginning of the pains I was to be feeling for the next hour or so. The only logical thing I could think of was that I was having a heart attack. Now I was in real panic mode and asked my boyfriend to call an ambulance; it was time for me to go to the hospital.

Where did this all come from? It happened on a Sunday afternoon; I was happy, content and enjoying my weekend. But my body and mind had other plans. They had accessed all the stored-up and unresolved issues from the moment I entered this Earth to that exact day. My emotions had an overload and they needed to escape.

Once at the hospital, I was given a CT-scan, and had some other tests, including blood work, done. I remember laying on that hospital bed, feeling incredibly scared for my life and my general wellbeing. Everyone was escorted out of my room, and I was questioned by a psychologist and doctors about my living environment, my family situation and similar general questions. They were trying to work out where the stress had come from.

I remember answering their questions vaguely and generically as my mind was on autopilot—it was like I wasn't really there. I felt like I had been on a massive adrenaline high and was just coming down from that roller coaster ride. My brain was complete mush. Besides feeling like this, I believe that there was a part of me that didn't know how to answer the questions they were asking anyway. Now, don't forget that these were the unconscious Natalie days—the days that provided me with experience to learn, develop and grow from. I did not have answers for myself, let alone a doctor or social workers.

Hours had passed before I was finally given my results by the doctor. "You didn't have a heart attack." Those words couldn't have given me more relief. This is all I wanted to hear. This entire experience was put down to a result of stress. Later that night, thankfully, I was allowed to go home. I remember feeling so weak and frail. I had the life sucked out of me and I felt emotionally depleted.

Unfortunately, this was the beginning of many panic attacks—there was more in there that had to come out. It was scary not being able to predict when they were going to happen; I felt completely out of control as it could happen at any given time. This led to feelings of isolation and feeling trapped in my own fear. My mind was living in scarcity, and I didn't know where to go from here.

I wish I knew back then what I do today; I wish I knew about all the amazing books and podcasts and natural and holistic practitioners. I wish I knew how effective yoga and meditation is. All in all, it wasn't meant to be for then; it was meant to be for now. Back then, it was all part of the process, and I am honestly grateful for it, truly. I choose not to be a victim to those circumstances and not to live in suffering. I always knew, on a subconscious level, that I would end up here, writing about it, hoping like hell that my story would someday help someone else that was or is in that exact place.

Anxiety, fear and panic attacks might put our minds and bodies through war, but we always have a choice, whether we want to continue to live in that place or we want to fight our way out and find the light to guide us home and to a better place. Accountability, consciousness, and love are what carried me out. Most importantly, it's in making the decision to do everything in your waking power to get yourself out, knowing that only you can do it and not relying on anyone else to get you there.

By all means, I encourage you to adopt a support team and to reach out and be brave enough to ask for help but know that those things don't get you over the line—you do. I knew that no matter what, I was the only one that was walking in my shoes, no matter how many people said they understood or gave me wonderful guidance and support. They are not you and you are not them. Start by stepping into accountability; it's the magic that sets you free and empowers the hell out of you—taking responsibility for what you are going through. What can you be accountable for? Having this approach will also guide you to likeminded people, likeminded help and support. Only victims hang around victims; eagles soar and fly with the many others they choose to rise up and soar across the skies with. You are an eagle; I am an eagle; we were all born eagles—we just forgot that. But we can choose to remember.

Finding The Healers That Looked Beyond The Band-Aid

I have always been a big fan of health care practitioners that dive deep into what the cause of the problem is rather than conventional doctors who suggest a quick fix. I believe that to get to know someone and their underlying problem, it takes more than a ten-to-fifteen-minute consultation. More than half of the time, you leave with some kind of prescription, or they give you a pill to take and tell you to be on your way. A quick fix is never a true fix. If you want the fast road of just dealing with it or the Band-Aid approach, as I like to call it, then you could potentially be supressing the issue, covering it up and you'll be forced to deal with the same problem later down the track. It may look and feel the same—sometimes worse.

My reasons for feeling this way are due to earlier experiences and events later in life when having my children, which I will share in detail in later chapters. The conventional doctors, got me nowhere and nowhere fast, nor did they guide me or help me out of any situation I have been in. Don't get me wrong, I'm not saying not to utilize their services, nor am I trying to portray them in a bad light; they have helped my kids when they needed to see a doctor for a simple cold or bumps and bruises if they had a fall. I am grateful to have them in this lifetime and there is a place for them for sure. For me and my health problems, though, my guidance was not to be found with that kind of health approach. It was to be found in integrative health and in a holistic approach—doctors that specialise in combining both natural and conventional medical therapies.

After experiencing a frequent amount of panic attacks and trying to cope with the anxiety, I was gratefully guided to visit an amazing doctor by the name of Dr Karen Coates. She specialised in woman's wellness, hormonal health and everything to do with the female body. She was beautiful and she was amazing. After my first visit, I was sent for numerous blood tests. Dr Coates tested me for what felt like everything, she was extremely thorough. After two weeks, my results showed that my adrenals were shot from having so much adrenaline pumped into them from all my panic attacks. My cortisol levels were terrible, my immune system was weak, my iron was borderline anaemic; she didn't know how I had the energy to get out of bed in the morning. My cholesterol was high, and I had a thyroid problem. There was a real bag of goodies in those results. And to think I walked out of a conventional doctor's appointment where he told me, "It's just stress."

As time went on, I followed Dr Coates' advice and was given natural health products that helped address all my concerns. My whole experience with Dr Coates was extremely pleasant and empowering. I believe that it's important to have a good relationship with the person that is guiding you on your health path. It's a completely vulnerable experience and one that you instil trust into. She introduced me into a world of health that felt right to me and my gut intuition. I will be forever grateful to her for seeing me for the person that I am, not just the health problems I brought with me. As time went on, she became my regular doctor. I returned for further check-ups and started to see my health as a priority and made the decision to never go back to that weak, frightened girl on the hospital bed.

Once my body was fighting strong again, our next task was working on stress management. This is where Dr Coates referred me to a man that I forever hold dear in my heart—Dr Gerry Flynn. Some valuable information Dr Coates shared with me was that she thought it very important that the patient be paired correctly with the right doctor. She knew what type of person I was and what my constitution consisted of; she therefore thought it was important that I was seeing a doctor that nurtured and supported the current state my mind was in.

I was then sent to a cardiac centre where I underwent some simple testing to reassure me that the chest pains that put me in hospital were just that—chest pains caused from extreme anxiety and not knowing how to deal with it. The doctor I was referred to was Dr Gerry Flynn. After receiving healthy and positive test results from my physical stress test, Dr Flynn, being the wonderful an amazing doctor he is, didn't just send me home on my way. He sat me down and took the time to look into my issue with anxiety. He asked me if I would like to be shown the process on how I could take control and deal with these anxious feelings as soon as they arrived. After feeling comfortable with not having to get into detail with any reasons why I had such high anxiety at a young age, we began my first session of what was the beginning of the start of my life.

Dr Flynn's exact technique and the approach he used to help me through anxiety would best be explained in his book, Imprints for Success. To be put more frankly, I found it very much like a mild form of hypnotherapy or even a form of meditation. However, I was completely conscious the whole time—lying down with my eyes closed listening to his voice.

The aim of being in a relaxed state meant I was able to access all the resources that were available to me—recourses that I didn't even know I had—the ones that were within me and had been there all along.

I was to think of a time when I felt safe. On the first visit, that was manageable; I had to think long and hard, but I got there. Once I had this feeling in my mind and body, I was to turn it up big and bright and really visualise and feel that feeling of safety. Once I had that feeling running through my mind and body, I was to clench my dominant hand into a fist—locking in all that goodness, that safety, the peace, tranquillity, and harmony into my hand. Once this was done, I could release that hand and relax that thought. I was to repeat that process with a feeling and a time of happiness, a time of confidence, a time of love, passion or romance, and a time of health, vitality and wellbeing.

Once I had locked in all these positive resources, feelings and emotions into my dominant hand, I could access them at any time of the day or night. They were accessible to me as soon as I needed them. Whenever I felt any anxiousness starting to resurface or creep up in the middle of a shopping mall or while I was driving or even being around certain people, I would just clench my dominant hand, make a fist and all the beautiful feelings of safety, peace, health and vitality, love, passion, romance and safety would come rushing in and take over that negative, grey, anxious bubble.

I had rediscovered all these beautiful moments that really did happen in my life. Connecting to my resources brought me back to every wonderful feeling I had within me. Feelings I had forgotten—beautiful memories I let fear take control over. It's reassuring to know I had it in me the whole time, and that I just needed to be shown the tools for how to access them.

This work took accountability on my behalf—a commitment to putting it into practise and an even larger commitment to myself that I would do everything in my power not to go back to my old ways and beliefs. I had been blessed with such an amazing support team of doctors; I didn't want to let them or myself down.

It always felt much easier to take the safe path—the path that didn't feel risky and daunting. You feel more comfortable and in control doing what you're programmed to do, what your pain body wants to do, and what you have been doing. This is not the path of freedom. Earn your freedom and do the work; you are more than capable of it—overqualified one might say. It's in you to escape and rid yourself of these untruthful feelings. It starts with a choice—one that only you can make for you. Do I really want to rid myself of anxiety, or do I wat to stay safe in my story?

This process took time; it wasn't a long time, but I went for regular visits, maybe about six or so visits. However, each time, it became easier and faster to find a resource to access. At the beginning, I couldn't even find a moment of happiness. I remember tears rolling down my face and apologising for not discovering them. I felt silly and embarrassed that I couldn't access something so simple.

After the second visit, I began to change as a human being as I slowly found what I was looking for. Things take time and, in their own time they will appear, if you surrender to what you don't have control over and simply trust. By the last session, I was a completely different girl—one that felt calm, reassured, happy and confident. Dr Flynn even noticed how I sat in the chair—I sat with my shoulders back and head high; I wasn't crouching or looking extremely introverted with a lack of self-confidence. One would say I even felt proud to be me. I had love for myself that I had never experienced before. I felt like a worthy human being.

On my final visit, I walked out feeling so much happiness, so much joy. I felt light and, most importantly, I felt truly free. My mind felt clean, and I no longer felt trapped by anxiety and panic attacks. When it came time to say goodbye, I thanked Dr Flynn with all my heart for everything that he had done and what he had taught me. Being the humble man that he is, he replied, "I didn't do anything, you did it all yourself." Despite his response to me, I knew it was a team effort. There is no way I could do this without him. His teachings saved my life. From that moment on, I have never experienced another panic attack. How cool is that? I can also say that I'm not an anxious person and I don't suffer from anxiety. I will forever be truly grateful for these two wonderful doctors for showing me the way and for investing time into me. I am relieved that we have doctors like this in our world today that are willing to look at other approaches to a person's wellbeing.

How amazing is it to know that there are doctors out there like him that are willing to look at other ways to deal with stress and anxiety without having to take medication or unnecessarily dive into the past? I love that I had to do the work myself in order for it to take affect and make the change. Quick approaches are needed when things have gone too far and have gotten out of control. If you can take responsibility for what you want to change, you will eventually change it. Take responsibility as soon as possible and let accountability drive you through your experience. It's only truly you that can help yourself at the end of the day. We can be guided by the best doctors, physicians, books and mentors, but if we don't action the information that has been gifted to us, then the whole problem is still left floating in the abyss, constantly waiting for us to deal with it, reappearing until we give it the acknowledgement it needs.

My Superpower Comes From Within

To this day, I can see, feel, hear and smell the moment I walked out of my last session with Dr Flynn. I was wearing a white dress with large, bright, shining silver stones around the neckline. I had worn my long, blonde hair out and tossed with a slight curl. I had ballet flats on my feet and carried a small bag with hundreds of little buttons on the front of it.

As I walked in between the cars, searching for my own, I paused and smiled from ear to ear. I decided to tilt my head back and take a great deep breath in and looked right up at the beautiful blue sky. I felt peace, I felt light, I felt joy, and, for the first time, I felt confident. It was incredible and a memory that I have never forgotten. I actually use this time, this vision and the feelings it brings with it as a resource in my everyday life. When I'm in need of self-reassurance or to shift my thought pattern, I clench my dominant hand and this returns to me and floods my mind with all the goodness this moment gave me.

Confidence was a very new feeling to me—one that I actually really enjoyed. Gerry Flynn would describe it as justified self-confidence as opposed to arrogance or fear-based confidence. My newfound confidence came from a place of self-love and reconnection to my true, authentic self. Gosh, life looked different; it felt different. Everyday was an exciting day with new adventures. Can you believe I even looked forward to the challenges? They never really seemed like challenges as I always felt like I had the situation under control. I can best describe this process like carrying around a remote control.

When there was a problem or a challenge, I could pause the situation and freeze the moment, giving me the time to process my feelings. I had time to think about how I was going to handle it best. I was aware of what emotions I wanted to surface, and I was able to control being triggered. Once I had this all sorted out, I pressed the play button and I responded to the situation at hand with such grace and integrity. There was absolutely no reactivity, nor aftermath of reactive behaviour. It was incredible; I would 100% call it my superpower. I would walk away feeling so proud of myself, therefore giving me another happy and positive resource, I could use when I was in need.

Over time, people began to notice the change in me, the confidence in me. There was a newfound strength and energy I radiated. I was warned by both of my doctors, however, that some people may or may not like this newfound strength in me. A lot of people are used to the old, conditioned, play-it-small-and-put-everyone-first, don't-speak Natalie. They were used to their version of Natalie—the one they could control and the one that fed their unconsciousness. When I first heard this, I thought to myself, "How interesting, I will take onboard the wisdom," not being overly concerned.

As time went on, it all became true. Although I found that the majority were not phased and were mostly very happy for me, the ones that were closest to me that relied on me the most were the ones that were not. They needed all of me to fulfill and complete all of them. Seeing me make time for me, seeing the joy on my face as I casually enjoyed everything and feared nothing was nothing but a raw feeling that they were not accustomed to. I was now not relatable to the unconscious mind. I was not relatable to a scarcity mindset or a negative one. What they seemed to forget was that, just because I no longer represented those qualities and was no longer stuck in that frame of mind, it didn't mean that I wasn't once there and that I couldn't understand it. I hadn't forgotten what it was like to be there. Life continually brings with it challenges that want to test my superpower. For some reason, again, I found people in my life that did not want me to succeed. My success, my joy, my freedom, and my detachment from fear triggered their pain body, supplied their egos with fuel to regress and self-destruct.

What they saw in me was not what they believed they had in themselves. In return, I was emotionally outcasted and spoken to like I was nothing more than a worthless little girl. "Who do you think you are?" was used to throw me off my healthy train of thought and bring me back down into self-doubt. When I became aware of what was going on and choose not to deal with the verbal abuse like I used to, I would quickly be manipulated into being told that I was a "disrespectful girl". I was even told several times that I was not right in the head. All this from people that told me they loved me unconditionally. My superpower couldn't really hold that hurt out. I still feel; I completely feel, and I never want to change that. It's part of what makes me who I am. How I choose to deal with those feelings is what determines my outcome. After all, it had only been a month or two that I had been implementing the new skills I had learnt. It was something I had to work on daily. Triggers were my invitations.

I will say, however, that it was sad that this happened and hits me hard when it comes from a so-called loved one. In my situation, the people closest to me were the ones affected by my change the most. I now look at it as a part of my life's journey—part of my ever-growing puzzle of self-worth. I remind myself that, on a soul level, I signed up for this life to learn, evolve and grow and not to repeat the same lessons in my next life. I can't deny that the words didn't leave emotional scars—they did. As you may have gathered by now, I'm not one to let them define me. I won't play the victim, no matter how many people don't like watching me grow strong and do the polar opposite to what they would do.

In all honesty, it was me that showed them how to treat me. I have shown them a version of myself that they were used to. They identified me with those awful, fearful, limited beliefs. They only know me as playing small. I gave everyone else everything and didn't give me anything. It's no wonder I shocked some people with this new superpower of self-worth. I am 100% accountable for showing them how they could treat me. As you're most likely aware, I was this way from a very early age. My responsibility today and how I cannot play a victim in this situation is to step up, value myself and not allow nor accept any form of abuse and ill will of any kind toward me.

When finding myself in a circumstance where people would project, this would be an example of my self-talk:

Just because I have chosen to love and value myself this way in no way reflects any form of disrespect in my character. The reputation that you want to create and portray of me is on you and you alone. I am not responsible for your thoughts or your unhappiness. I was not born to take on your lessons, they are for you to learn and grow from. What you seek to find in me belongs to me and is not yours to take and manipulate into a version that works best for you.

When you realise that you are your problem and you are your solution, you will see that I have nothing to do with any of it. I, Natalie, release my mind from believing any words that are spoken to keep me believing I am not worth the value that I find within myself.

People that truly love you don't treat you in ways that make you question who you are, even if they can't understand or relate. People that truly love you don't see your freedom as a threat; they want to encourage more of it. They want the best for you, always. People that truly love you want to see you succeed and live your best life, even if that means they don't fulfill theirs.

Although I had now accessed what Gerry Flynn would call my full potential, I had a to do my best to maintain it, and that took work and so much continual effort, but I did it.

The Beauty in The Eye Of The Storm

Life was different now and I could never go back to the way I was. I couldn't unknow, unsee or, un-feel what I had become. It was part of my purpose and my life's journey to go through everything I did and end up here, where I stand. Each day, I would wake up to a feeling of excitement. I felt untouchable, like nothing or no one could break me anymore. When a situation or someone would try to, I had my resources and my confident state of mind that would be available and ready to support me at any given moment. It felt wonderful to have complete access to my true self and inner being. I wanted to live like this forever.

This was a pivotal point in my life, and I credit it to everything I had gone through, especially to that defining moment on that hospital bed, remembering the grey, dark and frightened feelings that moment represented and making the decision that I absolutely won't end up back there. If I did, it would've been through lack of trying.

I have learnt that I need to be kind to myself and to love and value myself more and to trust my body's signals as forms of communication. I have learnt that I am not alone and that, unfortunately, thousands of other people have gone and are going through the crippling feelings of anxiety and feeling isolated because of it. I'm here to tell you that it's ok. You are not alone, and there is a light at the end of the tunnel if you want there to be. Anxiety keeps you in fear and makes you unconscious to what your true self is trying to inform you of, wanting it to go away and making a promise to yourself that you will do everything in your power for it to go away, even when you don't have the answers or know how.

Taking the first step of knowing you want more is the start. Make yourself non-negotiable. Make you matter because you absolutely do. Know that any feelings that don't make you feel joy, uplifted, blissful and loved are just trying to trick you and suck you into fear and keep you unconscious. You are a conscious human being that is capable of anything and everything. Now, that's not me trying to fluff up your feathers and write something generic. It is absolutely true. If you don't already believe that wholeheartedly, chances are you have forgotten and just need to remember, return to you and go within—it's there.

"Healing is an art of unlearning." I read this recently and got shivers. I love it and wish that I stumbled across it in my early stages of life. Unlearn the areas that you were taught what you should do instead of what you felt right to you. Unlearn all the learned behavioural patterns that brought you to your breaking point. Unlearn all the methods that keep you hidden from the true you that really wants to be set free. Unlearn all the toxic reactivity that kept you in a scarcity mindset.

It's ok to free yourself from what you know in order to be safe even when you know, deep down in your heart, that habitual way of thinking serves you no good. The easy road is to stay doing what you have been taught to do, perhaps even told how to feel and how to respond. If this learned behaver is working for you and your highest good, then, by all means, continue. If it's not, and it's someone else's idea of right and wrong and what they have adopted in order to survive, then my suggestion would be to get out of that way of thinking and find your way into your own heart and your own soul. It's there where you can be truly honest with yourself and those around you. Be authentically you. Rewrite your own program that works for you, that serves your highest good and fulfills your purpose. Unlearn what you know and learn what works for you. Take lessons from your soul; you have everything you need to know inside of you.

The absolute best time to start is when you are right in the middle of the storm. I use the expression, "You need to find the peace in the chaos." Realise you're in a storm and make the decision to get the hell out of there. Your true self doesn't want you to suffer; it just wants to grow and learn from what it is showing you.

We all have times in our lives when we're riding high up on a mountain top, enjoying the fresh air and the view from above. Then there are times when we find ourselves riding low, stuck in a gully, trying to find a way out. We all know this is the ever-growing circle of life—its ups and downs, highs and lows, changes and seasons, its polarity, one may call it. The question is, when we find ourselves in the gully, how are we going to handle it? What does our mindset look like? What are the tools we are going to use to get us out? Are we aware of our resources? We all need tools, recourses and awareness to get through the tough times. They come and they're coming—you know that, I know that. So, let's get a plan to help us survive it.

Today and every day, I choose to see myself as a big, tall Oak tree. I bend and sway in the wind, with roots set so deep that nothing can uproot me. I am no longer the small tree that gets blown around, losing leaves and branches and gets uplifted and destroyed by the storm. I do not see myself as weak and fragile. We all know storms blow over; they always do. Some last a lot longer than others and there is a purpose for that, even when it's hard to believe. I believe we are all solid, strong, magnificent trees. We were born to apply ourselves like this. Whether we were born into human bodies that already function this way or we were born into bodies that need to find their way there, either way, as a beautiful mentor of mine, Emily Gowor, would say, "We are born great and with purpose." I believe I was. I was absolutely born great. I just forgot I was.

I experienced a storm, believing I was a small tree with no roots imbedded into anything. I was a girl that grew up being uprooted and completely blown away into a land of uncertainty, fear and disbelief. Only to find myself washed up in a place I never want to be in. Once I was there, I became present with my surroundings. I became conscious and decided that I would never be put through a storm like that again. I learnt how to grow from a small, fragile tree to a strong, robust one. My ability to learn a new way of thinking helped me to create new strategies to handle life—a life that was unfamiliar to me—but, in return, helped me grow roots into a solid foundation I could trust and rely on, roots that were strong and would keep me grounded, tall and able to survive any storm that came my way. My tree is eternal and everlasting and cannot die. It holds wisdom, knowledge, power and love. After everything, I am eternally grateful to have discovered it, for I don't know if it would have been possible if I didn't have the storm.

Part 4
Love

'Like attracts like, and if it's not like, it won't last'

Anonymous

Having spoken so much about finding love from within, I feel it relevant to share the story of a love that has been the most significant to me in my life—a love that has both supported and encouraged my growth; a love that was built with no conditioning and provided an environment to express freely the soul I was born to be.

I feel it's essential to mention that underneath the surface of all relationships is work. The extent of that work is different for each one of us. I think it's important to see relationships as exactly that—work—and not something that you enter to mask or fill a void. To expect someone else to provide what you may be lacking within yourself is an enormous undertaking that is doomed from the start. I believe where you are within yourself determines what type of partner you attract and what type of relationship you accept. In order for me to be involved in a thriving one, I want to add to a relationship so it can grow, not subtract and take away from and suck the life out it.

Above all, when there is trust in a relationship, there are no limits to how far it can go, where it can be taken and what heights it can reach. With that trust, I allowed myself to discover new parts of Natalie, parts that I didn't know existed. I am forever grateful for the ongoing work that both my husband and I invest in.

The Night in The Ford Laser

It all began one night in the front of my newly purchased White Ford Laser (no, it's not like that). I had driven over to show my boyfriend my very first car that I had saved up for and bought by my own hard work. I was so proud of myself. I was a first-year apprentice making a whopping $4.25ph, even back then that wasn't adequate. Obviously, this was a second-hand car, but it was all mine, and it was so worth it. The joy and satisfaction I had inside of me was electric and I wanted to share it with someone that would feel the same. So, sitting in the front of my brand-new car with a guy that was as happy as I was made for a great night. We talked for hours and hours about property, investments, what we see each other doing in the future, money, our work ethic, saving, when we were to purchase our first home, real-estate, etc.—not the usual topics two young people in their late teens talk about. But we did, and we did it all night long. Super sexy, right?

Hours and hours passed and, as each one did, my excitement grew. I felt so energised hearing Matt's attitude and prospective on his future. What I especially found to be a complete turn on was the fact that he was explaining how he was responsible for achieving his goals, how he was going to rely on his ability and knowledge to get where he wanted in life. At no point was he speaking from entitlement or expectation. Gosh, I loved this guy already. I could feel admiration starting to grow and I knew from that point on that this moment in this car on this night would be a significant moment in the story of Nat and Matt. Ten years, a marriage and two kids later, it certainly was.

That night, we both got an insight on how we individually viewed life and how we go about achieving what we are after, how we look at situations and what our attitudes towards different circumstance were. That night, we both realised that we were responsible for creating the world we wanted to live in. We were responsible for the choices we make, and that if we want something, we were going to assist each other to achieve it.

Unlike myself, Matt knew his identity from a young age, never letting hierarchical direction disempower him. Matt believed enough in himself to speak openly and honestly about what felt honest and right to him. For example, from a young age, he stated that university was not the path he wanted to take; it did not align with what felt right and true for him. He knew that everything he wanted to achieve in life did not come from that place. Although he had spent some time feeling shame and guilt for not pleasing those of concern, Matt knew what felt right and what didn't, and he chose to honour that. Another trait that I admired about him.

As the night went on and the conversation turned to me, I remember feeling like it was so easy to open up and talk. It was nice to be heard and even nicer to feel valued for your outlook and perspective. There was a mutual sense of admiration that was equally being exchanged between us. To this day, I can honestly say that mutual admiration is still very present in our relationship.

As time went on, seeing each other turned into dating, which turned into falling in love with each other. In so many ways, I believe Matt was my reward for all the hard work I had done on myself and for finding self-worth. It wasn't long before we moved in together into a small, cosy one-bedroom apartment. Moving in together was awesome and I loved it. Besides receiving my driver's licence, this was my next big taste of freedom. Moving out of my home provided me with a space to call my very own—a space that provided me the freedom of my choices. I loved being responsible for me and everything I worked hard for. Matt took great pleasure in enjoying me doing so. He has never had an agenda; if I am happy, he is happy, and vice versa. We set up a good life for ourselves in that little apartment. It was small yet provided us with an overflowing amount of joy. It was here in this one-bedroom apartment where we began to plot out our future investments. It's here where we began to put all we had spoken about in the Ford Laser to use. It was time to put our money and aspirations where our mouths were, figuratively speaking.

1 Bedroom Unit With 3000 sqm Of Aspirations

Back then, pre-kids, we had the luxury of spending all our hard-earned money on ourselves. When I say "ourselves", I mean we spent our money on rent, bills, savings and what we had left was our spending money usually for movies, clothes and dining out. We love a good night out at a nice restaurant; we were and still are massive foodies. But I must let you in on a secret—we absolutely love saving. Yes, it's true, putting money aside, watching it grow, prosper and invest it—there is something so satisfying about it.

So, not long after that we decided to start saving as soon as possible for a deposit for our very own property—our first and one of many. Matt and I both wanted to get into the property market as soon as possible. The right time is always now. We wanted to get in as young and as fast as we could. With that, in mind, we needed to save a healthy deposit for our first home. So, we did, no questions asked. We both had strong, steady jobs, we made a good income and relied on nothing and no one.

We were and still are very calculated with our money; setting up a good foundation and system for us to withdraw and deposit frequently was essential. Equally as important as the system was the relationship we had with money and how we treated and viewed it. So many people state the fact that they are saving, but what does that mean to you and what does that look like? Having clear guidelines and boundaries were essential, so was being on the same page as your partner; you need to get that absolutely clear from the beginning if you want it to be a successful process.

Saving was exciting and exactly what we wanted to do. That didn't mean it didn't bring with it times of temptation and challenges. To be honest, it was a little tough at times being faced with the reality of having to say no to offers and adventures that presented themselves to us. Not being able to see the other side of the world was major, especially while we didn't have the responsibility of children. Everyone told me, "Travel young and while you can." I know, I get it, but in my personal situation, saving for my first property and seeing the world were not an option for me.

Realising that you can't do it all was all part of our process. Matt is from Poland and has travelled a lot as a young boy. So, travel wasn't a massive priority for him. To me, visiting other countries, seeing other cultures, ruins and just smelling the air outside of Australia was all I could ever dream about. I never got to travel when I was younger and now that I was of an independent age to travel on my own, I would have to wait a tad bit longer. Travel is essential to my soul and my growth as a human being. My traveling heart ached to own a passport, to be able to walk through customs and declare myself legitimately out of the county—free to explore life and to follow where my heart was being called to. Realising at this time in my life that it was not yet my reality, nothing took away my hope and willingness to one day achieve my goal of travel.

Unlike our friends, other family members and nearly everyone we came into contact with, we were not receiving financial help from family to speed up our entry into the property market. My journey looked different, and my path had sacrifices. And it just made everything taste that much sweeter when I got there. It was so tempting at times, when you can see the money grow in your account and wish that you could just sneak overseas for a just a little. This, however, was not the time. At this moment in life, we had to choose one or the other; it was never a matter of both, and that's ok.

No matter how hard or long this process was going to be, this was the beginning of a transformational process and one we would forever look back on and it set us up for life. This process of sacrifice and prioritising grew with it an attitude and outlook that cannot be bought. This outlook on life and circumstances has been the key component to the success of our financial and emotional relationship. For if we were handed things in life, I don't believe we would have achieved the same determined prospective on situations, events and life circumstances.

So, we needed to stay laser-focused—work and save and enjoy the simpler and magical things in life. My days of shopping at outlet stores and buying items of a modest price had continued for me and, like I previously mentioned, I think I was pretty good at it. I may be like some girls out there that love a good shopping spree. More so in those days when I didn't have kids. I find shopping for clothes, dresses, shoes, makeup, bags, perfume, jewellery, etc. so uplifting. I find shopping for personal items to be a representation of who you are. I found it as a way of expressing myself. I found freedom and acceptance in the person I was while I was shopping for Natalie. It gave me a lot of joy and reminded me who I was and how I can actually be a pretty cool person when you give me free reign. So, free-reign Natalie had to just put these things on hold a little longer or look for it in other places, which is exactly what I did. Besides, I was already accustomed to purchasing items on a budget.

Everything was a compromise, and our top priority was purchasing our first home together. It was a choice I made and one that was not forced on me. We were both very clear about that and there were no hidden feelings or agendas. Both our intentions and our vision were the same. So, with patience and persistence and a determined mindset, the magical day came when we purchased our first home. It was wonderful, exciting and it was all ours; we did it. We made it into the property market, and we now had a place to call our very own. This was the place we set up roots and marked the beginning of the next chapter in our lives. Goal number one, achieved.

The Mushroom And The Star

As I had mentioned earlier on, the process we underwent to save for our first property was the foundational system that was implemented for the rest of our lives. We created a structure which consisted of a strong mindset, clear perspective, focus, determination and, above all, internal support. This process was created because we had nothing and nobody to fall back on. We were never given financial lifelines or financial support, so what better way to receive support than to create it yourself?

In the iconic Nintendo game, Super Mario Brothers, Mario and Luigi, the two main characters, travel through the mushroom kingdom to save princess Peach. Along the way, they encounter challenges in which they are given these awesome lifelines called item boxes. Theses boxes are placed along their journey to help them through the tough times and any challenges that may lie ahead. Mushrooms make them grow and gives them another life so they can take more risks knowing that they have another to fall back on. Flowers allow Mario and Luigi to receive a fire-shooting device to clear their path of what is trying to stop them ahead. Finally, there is stars, which make them invincible and speed up their quest, knocking out anyone that stops them or puts harm in their way, they are a fast pass to the finishing line.

In life, there are people fortunate enough to have these item boxes placed along their journey. It's wonderful and to be celebrated. Like anything in life, there also exists the complete opposite; there are people that have lives where item boxes do not exist and simply put, were never an option. This was the case for Matt and myself; this is where the real magic begins and why I chose to discuss this topic in the love chapter. I honestly believe the success of our love has been in the lessons, trials and tribulations, and the adversity in building our own item boxes in our own lives. By doing this, we were able to develop one of the mind's most sought-after resources—resilience.

The process of having to build your own item boxes or build your own life raft meant that we discovered strengths in one another; the process highlighted each other's individual survival abilities. Like anything challenging and tough, it provides us a platform to learn from and find meaning to the pain or hardship. This experience not only brought resilience and tenacity, but the ability to see life through a different lens.

Take this as an example: Two teams need to get to the other side of a river. One team is gifted a prebuilt life raft while the other team must build theirs from scratch. Obviously, the team with the supplied life raft would get there first, as this bought time and a head start. The team who must build theirs from scratch will take five times as long, with no guarantees they will reach the other side.

So, I ask you this, which team do you want to be on?

Do you see the team that did not get a life raft supplied at a disadvantage?

It's nice to know that everyone will answer this differently, and there is no right or wrong answer—just a difference of opinions, and that's what make the world go round. I will, however, openly share mine, which is that both Matt and I are the life raft builders. At first, this obviously wasn't by choice, but after years of finding yourself in that position, you not only become very good at it, but you also start to see all the advantages that it gives you throughout all other areas of your life. When you build things from the ground up, you see everything that goes into it and all of what it takes. You get to witness the real-life actuality of the situation and all that's involved in it. It's like a backstage pass to reality.

You know how much you need and where to place it. You prepare yourself for unexpected outcomes and reinforce backup plans in case the outcomes manifest. You need to think outside your normal day-to-day capabilities and open your mind to a place that you may not have gone before. This may leave you feeling exposed and vulnerable, perhaps even doubting yourself.

Like in this scenario, it may not always look like a physical advantage, but, by far, it is an emotional and empowering one. What and incredible opportunity to be a part of, and one that would change the way we viewed any challenging situation we were to face in the future.

Becoming our own builders of financial stability has kept us humble and grounded human beings. I especially believe I was gifted this opportunity because, ultimately, life sends you the test you need most and mine is without a doubt self-belief. What better way to be tested than to be placed in a situation where you only have you and your mind to fall back on? When you think you have nothing to fall back on, you always have you. Even if you do not believe in yourself and think there is no way you can get yourself out of this, you can. We are always stronger than we give ourselves credit for.

I love my husband most of all for his perspective on life and his way of always being accountable for the situations he finds himself in. There is no such thing as blame—just invitations to higher ways of thinking and evolving.

I see value in being able to provide your loved one, friend, children or grandchildren with item boxes along their journey. I certainly want to be able to do that for my children. Although I won't be handing them out willy-nilly, a couple along the way won't take away from the many times they will have the opportunity to build their own life rafts, as that skill means more to us than any mushroom or star.

At times, it has been emotionally challenging knowing, time and time again, we have to go through the building process while others immediately get to start. It is in this time of emotional deflation that we must remind ourselves what this process will do for our mental strength and what it will add to our resilience muscle—it sure gets tested and worked out. We remind ourselves that, any challenges we face, we know that we can take the adversity and turn it into ways of thriving. And by doing this, we hope to be positive examples for our children.

During the time that Matt and I have been together, we have been asked countless times what makes our relationship what it is. The simple answer to that is, while building rafts, we build our love. What resources and supplies he is short of, I provide, and what I lack and cannot seem to place, he supplies. We work together as a team, and we rely on one another. I will always have his back, no matter if it breaks mine.

For me, personally, it hits hardest and hurts the most in two ways: 1. When Matt and I get told we are "lucky", and we just got to where we are in life because Matt has always had lots of work and he makes good money. 2. When you encounter certain naïve or entitled attitudes from those who have had an oversupply of mushrooms and stars and have never at all had to build a life raft of any kind.

These people always look for an excuse when they see someone climbing their way to that person's version of the top. Shallow assumptions come from an unconscious mind. It's a choice to be naïve as much as it is a choice to assume and not educate and inform yourself of the reality of the situation.

I often found myself wishing that they knew that luck had nothing to with it and that mindset, determination and never giving up had everything to do with it. On one hand, how could they when they had never been given a chance to be that second team on the side of the river? Yet, still, I have encountered many friends, clients and people that have not and still have a better understanding of the situation.

You do not just get handed a certain mindset; you develop one through the circumstances you are faced with. Life throws us all tough situations; if not financial; it's health, if not health, it's emotional turmoil and for some, it's all. It is my understanding that the people who choose to learn from these tough times, grow to evolve and achieve greatness because they never use the word "luck". We know that luck and resilience have nothing in common. Luck and a strong mental mindset have nothing in common. Luck is the language of the unaccountable. The word is often used to assign disempowerment to the person or bodies that have used everything but luck to achieve their goals and aspirations and to get to exactly where they have always dreamed to be.

I used to think, "If they only knew how little help we had, then perhaps they would see how far you can go when you have to rely on your own unique abilities and tap into strengths you didn't even know you had."

It has come to my understanding that the people that use the word "lucky" are the ones who have taken advantage of too many item boxes. They are the ones that have had an oversupply of mushrooms and stars. The people that have put their lifelines to good use and used them to get to where they are, do not see luck as something that contributed to their successes. I believe there is a big difference between help and an oversupply of handouts and cash injections.

Despite external images, we all have different financial experiences, and these images often have no reflection on what their true financial situation is. These experiences are due to the choices we make, the goals and dreams we set, the number of stars and mushrooms we receive along our journey and, most of all, our mindset and relationship with money. No journey is right or wrong, good or bad; simply different.

I would love to encourage you all to look beyond exterior images and dive into more detail when it comes to questioning what presents as successful or financially successful. Often, we are influenced by external façades as a way of defining someone's financial success—the car they drive, the business image on Instagram, the sunglasses they wear, the bag they carry.

In the UFC, there are several different divisions which include light weight, strawweight, Bantamweight, heavy weight, feather weight, middle weight. Each division has weight standards and fighters only face opponents in their same weight class. It would be a disadvantage and a completely different fight to put a fighter of a lower weight division with one of a larger division, for reasons I am sure I don't need to outline.

A major part of being a professional financial raft builder is knowing what weight division I'm in. It is to remind me that my division is not the same as others and that theirs is not like mine. We are all in different divisions and there is success to be held in each one of them, despite how many times you get knocked down or feel deflated.

Before any emotional deflation, I would not only remind myself of this, but also ask myself how many item boxes they had access to. How many mushrooms and stars were used in the making of this image? This helps me put my life into perspective and keeps me focused on what I need to achieve in my own division. Don't measure your success with those that have been given fast-passes and cash injections. It is an incomparable situation. We are simply not on the same path. We are on our own unique and awesome path that is extremely prosperous in its own way.

My nine-year-old son saves for his PlayStation games; he works hard washing the car, mowing the lawn and doing his household duties. Ashton's friend, on the other hand, only has to ask and it is given. We explain to Ashton that we simply have different rules in our house and that there is no right or wrong parenting; that we simply want to teach him the valuable lessons that saving money and being responsible can teach.

Ashton eventually saved for his PlayStation game. With this effort, focus and determination came a sense of pride and gratitude that Ashton found within himself. I could not buy this feeling for him; it was completely character building and a wonderful moment to witness. As the months went on, he would set new goals and by all might he would achieve them. This attitude reflected in all areas of his schooling as well. His teacher even pulled me aside and made note of telling me that Ashton had become such a responsible and reliable boy. He makes good choices and is always extremely grateful for everything he receives. This news lights me up. A few weeks after the PlayStation purchase, Ashton had mentioned to me that the friend that receives whatever he wants, whenever he wants, has no appreciation for his belongings. He just throws things around and has little disregard for what his parents have given him. He said, "Mum, I can tell he does not have to save for things, because he does not care about the things he has." He told me that his mum and dad would just buy him a new one.

It was a real eye-opener for our son to see how having the resilience and the skill to save and be vigilant with your money reflects in your persona. Having respect for money and gratitude for one of the most important resources this life has to offer can be the most valuable thing you inherit, and you need not get it out of an item box.

At the end of the day, we truly cannot compare ourselves to anyone. We do not know how much help they received to get there and how much of the life raft they have to fall back on. If you do not have any of this, please do not feel deflated. I know how scary, vulnerable and isolating it feels not to have that reassurance, that safety of knowing you are going to be ok and land on your feet when you take a risk. But you need to remember that you are stronger than you think you are—way stronger—and we were each handed an assigned life path. That path is individual and unique to each one of us and with this path comes some incredible gifts, lessons and experiences that are designed for us to enjoy learning and evolve.

We all get to where we need to be eventually because hard work, a healthy mindset and an accountable attitude place us there.

Colin, The Other Man in The Relationship

Our dear Colin, how much we love, value and adore you. We hold so much gratitude for all that you do for us. You never let us down and even when you are down and having a bad day, week, month, you always find a way to bounce back and keep on being magnificent and wonderfully supportive. You are a true legend.

Colin is the name we gave to our balanced index investment fund. That's, right we are those people—the ones that create a name for not only our investments, but our everyday accounts, bills accounts and saving accounts, along with names for our investment properties; my car even has its very own name.

The reason we do this is simply because we have strong relationships with all of them. They are like friends to us; we hold them dear and treat them with kindness and compassion. They are the life rafts we have created. We take the time to listen to them and learn how to respond to their queries. Before you call me crazy, ask yourself this, why wouldn't you name them?

The way we see it is that money is one of the most important resources you can acquire in this human lifetime. It is also one of, if not the largest, relationships you enter. It is the one relationship that is completely honest and truthful. Money does not lie, it's not deceitful, it's not emotional; it is simply a reflection of what you guide it to do. It's patient, it's kind and it is instructed by you; some women would think it's the ultimate guy.

Why not form a relationship with your most precious resource? I have always had such great love and appreciation for my bank accounts. This was an attitude I developed at a young age while I was working as a first-year apprentice. Once my body, mind and soul slugged it out in the salon, I made sure that what I was to receive for my efforts was not going to go to waste. When the yellow money wallet hit my hands, I knew it was now my time to be responsible and accountable with what I did with it. For it's not about what you make; it is more about what you do with what you make.

From day one, I had a plan to first pay for any bill (only a car and insurance at that stage), and second to put a large amount into savings and the smallest amount and what was left over I allowed myself to enjoy and spend it on whatever made my heart happy, which was usually clothes. Often, I would have to put aside this amount and wait until it grew enough to purchase a modest dress as I really didn't earn much at all. All in all, I had a system in place and structure to my very small income. This structure has evolved over time and, thankfully, has flourished. This system was created by me and motivated by me; I was never shown or guided to do it. This is just what felt right and, despite being young with low self-belief, there's one thing I have absolutely always had, courage.

I had the courage to do what felt right and set my earnings up so that I could fall back and rely on me if I needed to. As time went on, the financial system I set up benefited me in many ways; I managed to save for my first car. I was able to purchase whatever I needed to buy, even though it may not have been high end fashion. It never bothered me in the slightest; it meant that I did not have to rely on anyone. I was also able to assist financially those that were around me that needed it. Making money meant that I was one less person that anyone around me needed to worry about. For so much of my life I have felt relied on emotionally; it felt incredible to buy myself freedom and independence.

So, it was from this early stage in life that I discovered a love for the relationship of money; I loved the freedom it gave me. I learned that money would work for me if I gave it clear and easy guidelines to follow. It worked as my best companion when I realised that I was responsible for it. I was my money's voice. Learning this at a young age was pivotal in the story of Natalie and even more so in the story of Nat and Matt.

Little did I know back then, I would attract a life partner that had the same views and appreciation for this wonderful resource, and so began the late-night discussions in the White Ford Laser.

Money is energy and energy has its own frequency and vibration. If you're low-vibe, then you're going to make low-vibe decisions. If you're feeling awesome and riding high, then there is no doubt you're going to make better choices with what you do with your money. Money is a mindset.

We never blame the share market or the dollar when it drops because you know, if you are in the game, it is going to at some point. Your house decreases in value all the time; it goes up and it goes down. You just do not physically see the numbers going up and down every day, but it does and you're still in the game. Everything is not for everyone, but how you do one thing is how you do everything.

We all experience highs and lows with many aspects of life. Why do we get shocked if we have lows with money, too? It is a part of life and a relationship that we are invested in, whether we like it or not. Like anything else, as soon as we become accountable for the decisions we make around our money, the sooner we will see that what happens to it is nobody else's fault but our own.

Money lows, falls and rock-bottoms are all invitations to address where we went wrong, whether it be trusting that person in the partnership that failed or putting too many eggs in one basket and having it all gone overnight. I know what it is like to grow up as a young girl in a bankrupt environment and I also know what it's like to be older and make the wrong career decision, change jobs and wonder how you're going to pay your mortgage this month. I am absolutely no stranger to tough financial times.

What I take away and have always felt from a young age is that it's not a blame-game; it's an accountability game. The money was just doing what you told it to do. Be responsibly and own your part in the relationship you're in. The financial relationship we enter with money.

This is why I believe to my core that it is so important that we start young. As we learn to find love for ourselves, friends and family, we also need to find love and a good foundation for our relationship with money.

The way we reinforce our love, our frequency, our energy, with our money is by talking to our accounts as if they are a part of our family. "Oh, Colin, you're looking a bit down today; you've lost a fair bit overnight. That's ok, buddy, we all have sick days, and we all get better. We are here for you, buddy. We've got your back. We love and appreciate all that you do for us. We do not just love you when you're good and you have returned thousands to us overnight; we love you even when things are down." Overall, our relationship with Colin is a great one, so we choose to keep investing in it. If it wasn't, then we would make the responsible decision to end it. Like with any normal relationship, sometimes, things don't work out, and that's ok. At least you were in the ring, ready to fight. At least you got up off the sofa and gave it a try. You always create more momentum, more wonderful moments, went you get up and try. You're already a winner for trying, and the universe always rewards people that try and try again.

Together and individually, both Matt and I have many financial goals we wish to achieve; creating a good relationship with the thing that is going to get us there is essential for us to enjoy a prosperous financial future. Making constant mental wellbeing deposits and checking in on where we are emotionally is also essential for us. Taking responsibility when things did not work out, learning from our mistakes and making sure that we get back up if we get knocked down, are all massive game players to our mental financial attitude.

Finally, coming to the understanding and acceptance that it will only ever be us that we can ever truly count on has been the largest catalyst, which inevitably motivates us and pushes us forward.

That attitude determines how far we will go and how far we can go is endless.

Do You Want Your Man To Be Happy Or Present Happy?

My husband has a yearly "Boys Trip". He travels south to attend the ever-iconic Bathurst 1000 V8 Super car event held in New South Wales. He has been going ever since we have been together; I think it's great and encourage him to go every year.

Why? Simply because I love to see my man happy, period. When Matt is doing something that lights him up and fills up his cup, it floods through to my heart and makes me feel warm and joyful on the inside.

There is a big difference between seeing someone you love experiencing happiness compared to watching someone you love presenting happy, on the outside. Presenting happy may look like a smile on his face, a few short words describing his weekend and a quick sum up of "Yeah, it was nice." But is that how he truly feels or what he feels comfortable enough to express?

I have been involved in many friendships where my girlfriends had this whole tit-for-tat discussion going on. "Well, if he gets to go away, then I get to go away, too. If my husband gets a footy weekend, then I get a girls' weekend at a day spa." Now, although there is nothing wrong with filling up your own cup as we are all well aware of, I want to ask you this. Is it really called filling up your own cup when you are doing something to even out the score between you and your husband? How about he gets a weekend away, a boys' night out, or just some much-needed man time with his mates and we get to simply be happy for them?

This seems to be such a hard pill to swallow for some women. When I get asked what makes Matt and I such a strong couple, the simple answer is that I really want Matt to be happy; I want him to feel happy and experience moments of happiness and joy with or without me. Matt is an individual identity; just because he is my husband doesn't mean I own him. Controlling someone's right to experiencing joy in their life because we are feeling joyless is a form of mental abuse, not to mention it's completely selfish and unloving toward the one person you supposedly love the most.

Having the courage to admit that this rings true for you in your relationship is a great way to see what truly is bothering you about your partner experiencing happiness without you. It may be that you are struggling to find happiness in your own circle of friends, or perhaps you feel like you haven't received enough attention from your partner lately. Perhaps you feel tired and overworked and completely joyless. Finally, and what I find to be the most common cause, is that we don't have our own overflowing cups. Some of us need that in order to view our loved ones in a joyful light.

Whatever it may be, there is a perfect opportunity to dig deeper into this feeling and work out what may be triggering seeing your partner express or experience happiness.

If I were to look into why I feel so at peace with Matt's individual happiness, the first thought that would pop into my head is that he earned it, he deserves it and I trust him. I also love the fact that Matt doesn't rely solely on me to be "everything to him". I Don't want to wear that responsibility and I don't believe I nor anyone can be everything to everyone and still be a healthy and functional human being at the same time. Actually, I know this to be true because I used to try being everything to everyone, excluding myself, and I ended up in the hospital with extreme anxiety. I love that Matt doesn't look to me for all the things he can't seem to fill in his life. When I see him doing something lovely outside of me and our relationship, I feel relieved. I see his hobbies, friendships and interests outside of me as things to look up to and admire. Sometimes, I take note and implement his outlooks and approaches to my own life.

I'm extremely grateful that my husband is happy and feels safe and relaxed enough to express his happiness to me. It would be a real shame for him to feel otherwise. Presenting happy is external; feeling happy is internal. I signed up for an internal love that shines from within. It's my job to nurture what comes from within so that it will grow and flourish and flow into our ever-evolving relationship.

I Will Not Disempower One Gender To Empower Another

The number one rule created in my human heart and felt deeply in my internal soul is that "Thou shall not disempower one gender in order to empower another."

Emasculate – to deprive (a man) of his male role or identity; to make (someone or something) weaker or less than effective.

I have spent years of hard work and countless hours turning self-doubt into self-belief and choosing not to stay down when I was continually smacked to the ground by emotional abuse. By choosing to invest in myself and grow from the lessons life has given me, I consciously choose not to blame the one gender that was the crust of all my problems. This proves to me that I am a strong woman, and strong women don't blame and disempower they grow and rise and free themselves from the pain. They find ways to detach themselves from what no longer serves them and, most importantly, they don't rewrite the same story over and over again, keeping what did not serve them in the past into the now.

I feel strong in my relationship with Matt; I feel accepted, and I feel loved. However, like any relationship, we have arguments and disagreements. No matter how much of a storm we are in, there is absolutely no way we turn to gender disempowerment to fight back because we both see ourselves as equals in our relationship. It may or may not be your version of equal, but to us, it feels whole, complete and right and is our version of it.

Despite Matt's love for doing the laundry, cleaning, domestic chores, and being completely OCD, believe it or not, he is the more masculine one. I, on the other hand, love to gurney the driveway and build things, and I leave way more of a mess around the house. This doesn't mean I am not at all feminine; in fact, I wear the feminine hat in our relationship. We both possess both qualities in our relationship, despite which gender it comes from. An even bigger statement would be to say that I accept that there are simply things that Matt is better suited to do and there are simply things that I am better at doing. Just because I can learn and do them, too, doesn't mean I need to. I have nothing to prove to Matt or myself, I am always evolving and growing at my own pace—as is he.

To be honest, Matt can do absolutely everything and anything; he is one of those kinds of guys, and I'm sure there are women out there who can do it all, too. From painting a house to building a deck, fixing a car, home automation, scripting, coding, and yes, when I was learning how to perm, he could roll a perm rod better than I and still can (seriously, don't get me to perm your hair, get Matt).

Do I see this as a threat? Hell no. I admire how awesome he is; his abilities have saved us so many times in our lives and for people who have had minimal to no help, Matt on his own has been a wonderful resource to have. Is there anything he can't do? Well, yes, there is, and that is where I come in. I can and love to cook, and I believe I do it well and with lots of love and emotion. I am the heart of the home and I run my life and help run our three boys. I am their emotional support, physical support and overall support when they need it most. I am a mother, wife, friend and a Natalie, all in one.

We both have different roles to play, and we know what works and doesn't to keep our relationship thriving and functional. Who is the boss of the family? Who is the more dominant one? That answer is simple; it's either none of us or both of us.

Matriarchy – a system of society or government ruled by a woman or women; the state of being an older, powerful woman in a family or group.

Both Matt and I have come from very dominant matriarchic families. Living in a world where the pendulum is swinging to one side to try and create some form of equal balance, has meant that we have been a part of some extremely imbalanced gender dominance.

As I mentioned earlier, I see myself as a strong woman and I don't blame men for the way some of them behaved in the past, just as I don't blame woman for what they have done in the past and are currently doing to evoke power. Women are not weak, so we should stop viewing ourselves as that. For centuries, there lived many powerful women who have made their mark in this world. We do not live in a man's world; we live in the world that we create—the world that we choose to put ourselves in and be accountable in.

In our household, men are not the enemy; the enemy includes those that need to disempower one gender, male or female, to create power around another. Knock one down to build the other up.

I would never knock down anyone, let alone someone that I love and care about in order to be heard, seen or look like I am the more superior human. This approach resembles weakness and fear. It takes a completely powerless person to create such an environment.

Men are not the problem and woman are not the problem; blame is the problem and accountability is the answer. Look at the underlying emotions. What's underneath blame? Blame is what kids resort to; of course, it's also what a lot of adults' resort to at times as they can be the biggest children. Blame is a first response for some and for the unconscious, it is the last response. It has always been my conclusion that people that resort to blaming as their last and final response never grow, evolve and learn. They get stuck in a world fed by bitterness and resentment. When you can't allow your soul or your human mind to experience what it's here to do, you are slowly dying as a human being.

Blame will keep you locked in resentment and embraced in the darkness.

We live in a world where there is an oversupply of help and resources; there are many ways out of everything. It starts with us and has nothing to do at all with anybody else.

A Vision of Love and Freedom

As a young girl, escaping to my bedroom to dream or to place myself in thought was something I did often. It was there that I could have no restrictions on my thoughts or how far I could take them, or how far they could take me. It was in moments like this I would think about the future, it was times like this where I could escape the present moment. I could detach from what the world expected from me and slip into a moment where I was allowed to be all of me and more.

During this time, I would dream about freedom; I would think about the Natalie that I would like to become—the future version of myself. When given the opportunity to imagine the future, I would always see myself smiling, dancing, feeling overjoyed and confident with who I was.

I saw a version of me that I could not quite bring back with me here in the present moment at least not at this early age in time. It made me happy to know that no matter what I was dealing with or how I felt, I could always switch off and unplug myself from reality and go to a special place within myself and see myself in a worthy and loving light. In this place, I mattered. It was here where I saw the love that I knew one day I would receive and it's here, in this place, that I saw the love that one day I would find.

Upon returning to reality, I would wake up with a sense of regeneration and newfound sense of belief. I would hold faith in my heart that one day what I saw and what I felt would someday come true. I never stopped believing that such love would find me, and it eventually did.

A dream is a wish your heart makes, when you're fast asleep.
In dreams, you will lose your heartaches.
Whatever you wish for you keep.
Have faith in your dreams and someday, your rainbow
will come smiling through.
No matter how your heart is grieving, if you keep on believing,
A dream that you wish will come true.

-Cinderella

Oh, Cinderella how I can feel your heart? Despite the environment you were in and how you were treated you never once stop believing that there was a love out there that would see you for who you are and love you for the person you are. It would have been easier to give into despair and give up, but you did not. Your attitude, your mindset, your songs kept you from falling into a victim and negative mindset—a mindset that Prince Charming nor the Fairy Godmother would have been guided to. It takes true courage to look beyond the darkness, to push past the hurt and to keep believing that you are worth more than the surroundings you find yourself in.

One of my all-time favourite mottos I live each day by include, "like attracts like" and "who you are reflects the kind of person you end up with." If Cinderella's heart were not so honest, loyal, hardworking and pure, then she would not have attracted a man that was all of those things. I try to be all the qualities I wish to receive, because reality is that if I am not the most amazing person I can be then, I cannot expect to attract that in another.

So, I am going to be the most amazing person I can be, in spite of what knockdowns life and people throw at me. My prince exists in my life because I never stopped believing that unconditional, true love exists.

Matt and I are two people flying together as one in this world called Planet Earth. We have highs and we have lows. We fight and we have fought. We are not perfect nor enlightened, despite what some very loving and completely biased friends may say. We are still learning and are students in the same class that we are all in—the class called life.

We do not know what the future may hold for us and, to be quite honest, we do not care because we don't live in it. We live in the now and the now is where our hearts lie.

Matt, thank you for loving me with free will and not enslaving me to your emotional needs. Thank you for allowing me to be emotionally free and to provide me a life where I can be not only emotionally free but all that I was truly born to be. Thank you for showing me that it's safe to be an eagle, that I will still be loved and accepted no matter what heights I reach and how far I grow. Thank you for being the eagle in my life.

Part 5
Becoming A Mother

Mother – a selfless, unconditionally loving human that never ever gives up on their child.

B ecoming a mother was such a profound part of my life. Are we ever the same person once we birth life into this world? Once we raise and parent children? Like everything in this book, it was very important for me to open up all parts of my personal experience as a mother; pregnancy, raising children, becoming a school mum and, most importantly, all the dark roads I fell into along the way. I was completely blindsided by all of it. But like anything in this life, it built resilience and made me stronger. I have never seen life the same way again.

Having Kids Will Be Like Raising Our Pets, Except, It Will Be Nothing Like That. Pets Are So Much Easier.

I remember this significant moment in life just before I had chosen to enter motherhood. I was 25 years old, working at a job I loved, and just moved into my first home, married the man my soul aligned with. I had gone through so many years of self-work, building a strong sense of who I was and who I had become, no longer feeling weak and insecure. I was running with a strong self-belief tank that was full and accessible at any time. I had spent what felt like my whole life working hard to get myself to this very point. I can honestly say I was the beast version of myself that I could be. Life felt good, everything was on track; I was on track, emotionally, physically and mentally, and so was Matt. It seemed like the most logical and fitting time to begin our family.

So, just when you think you have it all worked out, life gives you another case to crack. It was time for another huge life lesson coming in the direction of Nat and Matt. Boy, was this one an eye-opener. I wish I could have stayed in my riding-high moments, my I've-got-it-all-figured-out moment for so much longer. I was getting comfy and cosy with that feeling. But life and the universe had other plans for me. It was time for me to open a door that will never ever be closed. A door that I'm still working my way through; a door that leads the toughest, strongest, most courageous, the "I've got all my shit together, I'm the best version of myself" type of people to their knees. That, my friend, if you haven't already shouted it out, is called parenthood.

The Ultimate Test

Talk about the ultimate test of everything. Imagine the largest, most heaviest book you can think of, too heavy to even lift. Picture that book thrown directly, smack-bang at the middle of your forehead, knocking you for a sixer, only to recover, shake your head and take another massive hit. At least, that was what it was like for me. Wow, I did not see that coming. As we all know, there is no actual rule book for life; you completely have to rely on your internal self-belief system. It's either that or the 1.2 trillion opinions of other parents that have no better idea and are telling you what worked for them. In theory, this can seem helpful and super kind but, unfortunately, no two children are the same; they may be similar but nobody else is in your exact shoes. Connecting to that gut intuition, what we were all born with will eventually guide us to where we need to be and what we need to do.

Becoming a parent is life changing, no matter who you are; it changes the way we view life forever. I don't believe we even remain the same people anymore, good or bad; it's such a significant event. I don't know how you could look through the same eyes once you have grown a human inside you, once you have welcomed a child into your life and have seen a little person that has the makings of you. You created life! How amazing is that? Pretty amazing, if you ask me and equally as amazing if you have adopted a child or children into your life.

What I love about this process of creating life is that it celebrates the equal magnificence of both the male and female. For without one, the other wouldn't exist or be able to co-create. No matter which way you go about it—artificial insemination, all the many forms of IVF, surrogate, adoption or traditionally—you needed something from the male and something from the female to result in the most amazing bundle(s) of joy you can ever receive. How amazing is life and how amazing is the fact that we have evolved so far to be able to provide other ways to become pregnant and receive such a special gift?

I have been blessed to receive two absolutely beautiful and healthy boys. I am extremely grateful every single day of my life for having them in it. I wear the hat of parent proudly as I know it does not come easily for everyone.

It is my firm belief that for us to further support one another as women, as mothers and as humans, we need to first be honest with ourselves. We need to be honest with how we are feeling and what the truth of our new reality looks like. We must be courageous enough to use our voices and speak our truth and speak about what is really going on, what our story really looks like—the good and the bad. If more of us are open and real about what it has been like being a mother, than less off us would feel so alone and isolated; we would feel normal, loved and we wouldn't feel like we are failing. I know one thing is certain—on this huge, life-changing journey of parenthood, we all fall, some further down than others. No matter how dark your mind may take you or how numb you may feel to happiness, you are definitely not alone—I can assure you of that with every cell in my body. I have listened to many women open up in the salon chair and have had many friends open up about what their experience was like. This took courage, honesty and integrity to speak up and share. My intention is to do the same; by sharing my story, I hope that it will be the comfort and the reprieve to someone's feelings of loneliness and helplessness. You are not alone! Let me share my story with you.

Round 1- Unexpected King Hit

Thankfully, becoming pregnant, staying pregnant and having a highly functional and energetic pregnancy was in the cards for me. I had no sick days with my first pregnancy; everyday was a joy. I really enjoyed dressing up and looking nice while caring my baby bump. I loved wearing heels while being pregnant but did not love the eyerolls I got when I walked past certain people. Standing in line at the bank, they would openly say, "I don't know how you do it with those heels."

Like with everything else, when you have a pregnancy bump, it automatically means that everyone else has the right to throw their opinions and agendas right at it. I openly and calmly (on the outside; on the inside I was completely triggered) smiled back at them and replied, "Oh, it's easy. I just put one foot in front of the other and keep on walking." Little did they know that that was the last time in what feels like a million years that I wore heels on a weekly or monthly basis. Heels turned into sneakers, which turned into flats.

Getting accustomed to people's opinions was just something I was going to have to deal with. I love advice and helpful tips, but they were few and far between. I got more rubbish and negative stories; what I was going to be missing out on and how my life was going to go downhill. Not in a constructive way, but in a kind of bitter and resentful way.

At the time of my first pregnancy, I was working at a hairdressing supply store. People would come and go and leave their two cents whether I wanted it or not. The day came where I had to draw the line. One day, a lady came in and asked me if I knew the sex of my baby. I had just come from finding out the day before that I was having a boy, and I was so happy and elated. I told her I did, but we were not telling anyone as we wanted it to be a surprise. She replied with the most appalling response, "Well, if it's a boy, I don't want to know." She then made a face and said, "Boys... are disgusting. I couldn't deal with them. I have five girls and they're wonderful."

I was in complete and utter shock; I stood there and didn't even know how to react. I wish I could have, but I felt something boiling inside so if I did catch a breath, it would have unfortunately been a reactive reply. I walked back to my desk and felt sad and dumfounded. Who, in their right mind, would say such a thing? She was a mother! She had children of her own. How can she call any child disgusting? That was my limit; I turned to my very supportive boss and asked her if I could make a sign and place it in front of my desk. She agreed and the next minuet a, 'Yes I'm pregnant no opinions needed thank you!' sigh was created and placed on my desk. It was evident that if nobody had anything nice, helpful or constructive to say, then it would not be welcomed. The sign worked and I was proud of myself that I had the courage to create a personal boundary.

So, despite the unnecessary opinions, pregnancy was going well until it was "go time" on the first day of week 38. It was a Sunday morning, around 7:30 a.m. and we had spent the night before at the hospital. I remember walking into the delivery room to use the bathroom. As I walked in, I saw the bed on the right I was expected to give birth in at any time. As I walked past it, I smiled and chuckled to myself,

"There is going to be blood and guts on there soon." Such a weird thing to say, I know, but the bed looked so clean and white; surely, it would not stay that way after birth. I remember feeling strong, nervous and excited as this was my first time and I really didn't know what I had in store. I tucked myself in, not knowing it would be my last night's sleep in a very long time.

I woke up early in the morning; nothing happened overnight. I was still 2 cm dilated and had a few minor pains, but nothing I couldn't sleep through. My wonderful doctor walked in at around 7:00 a.m., all dressed in his golf gear. It was "go time". After settling me in and giving me reassurance, he was off to play his game of golf and said he would be back later. I always assumed the first child took at least twelve hours minimum of labour, so I wished him well and good luck on his game.

I was left with the most beautiful and amazing midwife. She settled me in and made sure I felt comfortable and relaxed. Within moments, I started to feel intense pain—paralysing pain. It came and went quickly. All I could think of was that if this was the start of my labour pains, and I have a long way to go, how I was going to cope. I imagined myself being a lot stronger than this. I was disappointed. I had a day of pain planned; I didn't envisage seeing me cave at the starting line.

I really wanted to do this naturally, as I truly believed I could, and I was also petrified of the epidural and really didn't want one (kudos to all of you who were brave enough to do it, I really admire you). My pain was intense; so intense it knocked the wind out of me. I sat on the bed and said to my midwife, "I'm in so much pain; I don't think I can stay like this for much longer. I can't believe I'm only 2 cm." Suddenly, I felt like I had to push, so I said, "I need to push," to the midwife. She looked at me and said in the kindest and sweetest voice, "Oh, honey, you wouldn't need to push now. It's too soon." She thought I was so innocent and naïve; bless her. She asked me to lay back so she could check, and at that moment, I saw her head lift and the colour of it was white and in shock. "You're 10 cm dilated; you're going to have a baby." She yelled out to the nurses to call the doctor back in. He even thought the nurses were playing a trick on him. "No, she is really in labour; you need to get back here ASAP." The next minute, he was by my side; he only made it to the car park and hadn't even left yet. "Sorry I made you miss your game," I said. "That's ok," he said. "No worries."

At 9:11 a.m., our beautiful baby, Ashton, was born. The smell of a new baby and the warmth of their little body on your chest, heart to heart, is really something you never forget. It really is one of life's most magnificent experiences.

So, how's childbirth? Well, intense. How amazing is it that we, the female race, were gifted with the ability to do such a thing? This is what we need to remember and remind ourselves that we're capable of. No matter how your birthing experience was, you are undoubtably the most courageous human for going through it.

Colic And Reflux, The Unacknowledged Soul Destroyer

Hours after my birth, our little Ashton was calm and quiet, he didn't come out crying and he was classed as healthy with no underlying conditions. The next day was when it all began. The undiagnosed, completely overlooked and unacknowledged, silent soul destroyer—colic and reflux.

This was undoubtedly the beginning of one of the toughest and most brutal stages of my life and, of course, Matt's life as well. Our baby was crying uncontrollably; we did not know what the hell was going on. We fed him, we changed him, we tried everything to get him to sleep but nothing was working. I believe he slept for a three-hour period somewhere within a 24-hour period. The rest of the time, he was in tears, screaming, crying and completely beside himself. It was torture at its finest.

Sometimes, he would fall asleep while I was feeding him. I just wanted to put him down so he could continue to sleep, but I had to burp him first. Our sweet little baby spent more time screaming and crying uncontrollably than being settled and content. The nurses eventually had to take him because they could see that I was a walking zombie, paralysed with fear of not knowing how to help this new little baby. My hormones were all over the place; no sleep and a screaming baby, a constantly screaming baby. I did not know what to do. All I wanted was to sleep so I could get my head around what the hell was going on. My body was not healing, and my mind was being blown apart. It was on constant fight or flight.

All the doctors at the time kept telling me that he was fine, his vitals were fine, my breastfeeding and everything looked textbook great. They said get ready for it, "He's just an unsettled child." Those were the words that I was going to have to live with for the next however long. Clinically, nothing was wrong; emotionally, everything was wrong. Unfortunately, my emotions were on fight or flight overdrive and my hormones were everywhere. I was beyond sleep deprived; I could not seem to make sense of any of this and connect with my internal mum compass. I was a mess.

As I returned home with this so-called "healthy baby", I returned as a different woman. I was no longer the Natalie that I walked in as. I wore a foggy, grey haze over my eyes. I carried a heavy chest filled with heartache, grief and pain of not knowing what to do, all while being assured that nothing was wrong with my baby by the professionals. Ok, so this is just what it must be like to have a newborn. This is normal, right?

Days and weeks had passed. They were all beginning to roll into one big, grey, dark ball of tight stress. The screaming was not subsiding, no matter what I did. As time went on, I made the decision to take him to a specialist. But no matter what specialist or doctor I saw, they would all say the same thing—"he's just an unsettled child; it's just colic and reflux." "Are you breastfeeding?" "Ok, good, everything is fine then."

I was now living in fear and riddled with it. All self-belief and listening to my internal intuition had faded away like dust in a windstorm, it was gone. I was now living unconsciously paralysed by fear and living externally.

Operating from the outside meant I chose to seek help from mainstream resources, anything that was common and easy to access quickly, like government-provided nurses and generic mainstream doctors. I needed answers and a quick fix, and I needed it yesterday. I was in such a state that I didn't stop and listen to the one voice that would have guided me to the right help, and that voice was mine. Instead, I settled for quick, fast and easily accessible approaches—people that just wanted to tell me that because I was breastfeeding and not giving him a dummy to self-sooth, everything was fine and normal, and I was doing what the textbooks at the time were saying was right. A one-size-fits-all world seemed to be the advice being served up and I was either to take it or continue to suffer. I would walk away feeling slightly worse than when I went in, if that was at all possible.

Let me get one thing clear, colic and reflux are not small issues; they are catastrophic, life-changing, challenging, isolating, cruel and unkind illnesses. They are completely overlooked and accepted as normal by our society. Why people in the medical world give no urgency to this matter is beyond me. So many people mistake a baby throwing up for reflux and think it's a small issue; some may say it's very common. It can be a small issue, but reflux and colic are not. I can tell you there is a massive difference. There are different levels of severity of reflux and silent reflux is one of the worst.

To be unsuccessful at soothing the un-soothed is one of life's most soul-destroying experiences, especially when you love them more than anything in this world.

Matt eventually had to return to work, so my days looked like hell on a stick, to be quite frank. Screaming followed by excessive screaming, followed by trying to get my baby who was overtired, overstimulated and probably hungry because he threw it up all over my body, to get any form of sleep was what my daily life looked like. I remember, one night, he cried from 9:00 p.m. to 3:30 a.m. Red-faced and sweaty, we couldn't calm him down; it was unbearable, to say the least. We were on the phone with the hospital when they asked us a bunch of questions, none in which they thought were red flags. They asked if I was a new mother and summed up their case with that information. Matt and I looked at each other, then looked at our bed, then at our screaming baby in our arms and said, "What have we done?" There was no going back, though; we had no choice but to see this thing through, no matter how much effort and absolutely no result we were getting. We were doing this all on no sleep. It was a living nightmare and one that never seemed to end with no light at the end of the tunnel.

If I was to ever so slowly saw my hand off, it would be less painful than watching someone you love so much suffer and not know how the hell to fix it; to wake up exhausted beyond human measure and have to find the capacity to think about how you're going to find yet another way to help this innocent child, all while he is screaming nonstop. So, sawing your hand off may sound dramatic, but I stand by the analogy. It's excruciatingly agonising.

As time went on, we looked for absolutely anything that would give us the slightest of reprieve. One day, we were presented this magical and helpful super device called The

Egg Swing. This was a device built for babies to nestle in. It would swing side to side, playing beach or forest music, with a small toy mobile hanging overhead. It should have been renamed "the saviour swing". When we put our little Ashton in it, he would fall asleep instantly as the constant rocking motion would send him off to sleep. Not for long, though, only about twenty to thirty minutes, was usually only one sleep cycle. But back then, twenty minutes felt like five hours. So, we had finally found something that worked; a slight loosening on the chest had begun only to be replaced with the advice of the nurses that we should absolutely not be using this. We were informed that our baby will develop bad sleeping habits and rely on constant movement to put him to sleep.

Inject more tightening to the chest and ramp up that fight or flight. Everything that seemed to help us and give us the slightest break, we were told it was bad for the baby and would create a rod for our backs. We were told by everyone close to us to give him a dummy; they like to suck, so when they have an upset stomach, it soothes them. I really wanted to and, eventually, I did, but with extreme guilt and shame as the nurses and midwives from the hospital did not want me to be using one. Apparently, they create teeth problems; they don't know how to self-soothe and they won't know how to self-regulate.

I just wanted to do what the professionals were telling me. After all, I have always been a girl that does what she's told. I trust people in their profession, and I would work hard to achieve what they recommended. I believed they knew what was best for my baby—not me (which was fear talking and me not trusting myself). I would, however, never make such a comment these days. Can you see all the red flags there? Living in this fearful state of mind, I put all my worth—or what I had left of it—into believing what the professionals said worked for the majority. Big mistake and lesson number one. I needed to identify that neither me nor my baby were the majority and there is nothing wrong with that.

I was a first-time mum and had unfortunately lost all the self-belief that I had worked so hard to gain. I had given all my power away to the professionals. I was a lost solider that had forgotten that I was a solider in the first place. I certainly was a soldier walking into that hospital, but what I left as was a weak, deflated, hopeless girl. If only I knew that having a baby was one of the most important stages of your life to access your self-belief system. You can take advice from the professionals but, ultimately, you are the only person that knows your baby better than anyone else. I wish I had of believed in myself more back then.

As my weeks somehow seemed to carry on, I would continue to visit nurses for regular check-ups as I believed this was the right thing to do, and I at least wanted to get that right. Each visit, I would explain the suffering and pain both myself and my little one were experiencing and got told the same thing over and over again—he's putting on weight, he's gaining, and he looks healthy, he's just and unsettled child and he needs to self-soothe. Anything that would help me, I was told not to do; it was a living nightmare and one that I couldn't get out of. I made the hard decision to send our baby to sleep schools. But even they couldn't help him.

I would start each day feeling heavy and all the shades of grey you could imagine. There was absolutely no light at the end of this tunnel. I had begun to lose my sense of direction, my sense of self. I had found myself returning to the old parts of me where self-belief and self-doubt had returned. Days turned into endless hours of torture where I would feel my body beginning to shut down and switching to survival mode. I remember feeling like it was unsafe for me to drive as I couldn't concentrate. I was meant to be enjoying this new stage of life of being a mother, but I absolutely wasn't. I was completely unhappy and beside myself, overwhelmed with fear, shock and exhaustion.

I made attempts to have a shower in the morning put on some half-decent clothes and brush my hair. I would make sure I wouldn't look myself in the mirror as I was too depressed to see the girl staring back at me. I would attempt eating but couldn't stomach it. I only ate for survival, to put nourishment into my human body so that our son would thrive. I didn't care that much for me; I was just a machine used to keep the baby alive. It didn't matter how I was doing, just as long as I was doing well enough for the baby's sake.

This was a major societal issue that needs addressing in my opinion. How the nurses and doctors could sit there and see the mother burnt out to the ground and carry the appreciation that it's all for the greater good just baffles me. Mothers need more help; we are the vessels of survival for the child. Sure, it's about the baby, but it's all about the vessel that brought them into this life as well—the vessel that's trying their hardest to do right and keep this baby healthy and thriving while still being a wife, a friend and a person, too. How about at the nurses do motherly check-ups to see how the mother is going each week, at each stage each month. Record the mothers' growth, weight, and physical and mental wellbeing. We are just expected to grow a human, birth that human, raise that human and heal automatically along the way. This is unrealistic and a very outdated approach.

Our mothers before us did it, so we are expected to do it in this completely different and new generation. What worked back then may or may not work for us in this new world. We are different women and the women after us will be different from us, too. You simply cannot compare different generations nor bring the same structured mindset into every aspect of this generation and to the women that are learning how to and becoming mothers today.

Yes, I can personally say I highly value a lot of traditional ways of mothering that have been passed down, but there are also plenty that I do not. Hearing the words, "Back in my day, we didn't have this, we didn't do that, we did it like this," is just hearing your story and your way of doing things. This was great for the mothers in that time, and I'm sure they, too, were doing the best they could. These words are all constructive and helpful as long as they don't have an agenda and a superiority about them. I ask this question of those that have come before us. If you were to give birth today, in this day and age, would you do everything exactly the same as you did it generations ago?

What I have found when it comes to mothering is that there is no right or wrong since there is no rule book. It's about what is right and wrong to you. So, when we let too many outside opinions come in the way of what feels true and right to us, we get lost, no matter how loving they might be. When we are lost, we can spiral down many different paths. We also must acknowledge that we need to do the work to put us back on the right path again.

Do I believe our mothers did it? No! I believe they did it to the best of their ability because I don't believe we can actually achieve it. We put too much pressure on ourselves to achieve it. We can all do our best, and some succeed at it better than others. But to get it right, to nail it, to me, it simply means the ones that try and never give up. The mothers that keep working at it when they don't know what else to do, and when there seems to be no light. The it I'm referring to here is a mother that absolutely never gives up; no matter their age, they never take their mother hat off. Mothering is constant work, every single day, until it's your time to leave this Earth.

Quitting is not an option!

Never Giving Up

At the three- to four- month mark, the colic had thankfully begun to subside. Before this point, I had made a conscious effort to implement a daily and night-time routine. I figured that even though there was more likely a huge chance of our baby not following it, I felt a sense of reprieve and direction that came from the slightest chance that it would work. So, religiously and without any influence, I put my head down and jot down a routine that both Matt and I would follow precisely. Whatever parts of me I had left, I begun to draw up a plan of attack, a plan to hopefully get some form of control of the situation. Nobody could help me, so I chose not to keep waiting around and I chose to do something about it.

I started by creating a bath time routine, although I had done this from day one since the hospital, I now began doing it the same time, every single day. After the bath, I would feed him and read him a book, then wrap, swaddle or put him in a sleeping bag to bed (depending on what age he was). I would black out the room and yes, I chose to give him a dummy; at the time, I felt very shameful about it, but chose to wear the shame, as Ashton seemed to love the dummy and I simply wanted to see him happy and content. This sleep routine happened every night at 6.30 p.m. and lights out by 7:00 p.m. We even named it "The Shut Down".

At first, Matt or myself would sit with Ashton with one hand on his tummy (he couldn't see us so it was just so he knew we were there). This process started with horrific screaming for what felt like hours (nothing new there), and it eventually went down to 45 minutes, to 30 minutes, to 15 minutes, to eventually little Ashton just going to sleep without us. It was a miracle; no, it was actually hard work and determined parents. When we first started this process, I remember crying, feeling overwhelmed, feeling like it was yet another wishful attempt. Tears would roll down my face while telling him everything is alright, and that mummy loves him. Deep down, I didn't know if what I was doing was right; I just knew I had to be strong and remind myself that he is loved, he is safe, bathed, fed and warm. I had to stop and remind myself of all the things I was providing him instead of all the things I felt I wasn't doing right. Looking back, the poor little fella just needed some structure.

Once Ashton was asleep, I would walk out of the room and what we call "the silent night" had begun. Matt and I lived in a small, two-bedroom townhouse (our first home), and you could hear everything. Once we knew he was asleep, we would barely even breathe. We were petrified that he would wake up start screaming and have to do all that all over again. We put socks on so it would be quieter and so he couldn't hear our footsteps; we made sure we ate dinner before the shutdown, and we didn't bother cleaning the kitchen as it would be way too loud and would guarantee a wake up.

We made sure we opened any doors we had to, so we weren't opening and closing doors while he was asleep. Heck, we didn't even want to flush the toilet. We pretty much got ourselves ready for bed before Ashton so that after the shutdown, we just went to bed or watched TV on two levels up from mute. Extreme, right? Back then, I would do anything for sleep; I would do anything to have a shower or be able to go to the bathroom. It was one time I could step away and be in my own body, my own head and I could do it guilt-free. Because hey, everyone's got to go.

Although this horrific stage in our life seemed to last forever, it obviously didn't. So, living like silent pixies eventually did end at night after several months. Daytime, however, was a completely different story. I know all you mothers out there get it when I say the days are long and a baby that doesn't sleep during the day makes for a very intense day, especially with one that has reflux and is unsettled after every meal.

Thankfully, my nights were beginning to look better. Ashton slept for twelve hours, 7:00 p.m. to 7:00 a.m., every single night. Sometimes, he would wake around 5:30, but I made sure I never went in until 7:00 p.m. Ashton was never screaming, though; he was just talking and occasionally a few tears, but nothing at all like his usual wail. I chose to stick to my guns and only enter at 7:00 a.m. Despite being told how "lucky" I was that my kids slept until 7:00 a.m., like everything, luck had yet again nothing to do with it. This took hard work, determination and persistence to keep this up as it would have been so much easier to cave and just go in. However, I stuck to my guns and knew that keeping him in his bed in a calm, unstimulated environment would benefit him, and I knew that as soon as I got him up, for the next twelve hours, he would not have a proper sleep until night-time came again.

At 7:00 a.m., I would burst open the door and begin to sing, "Good morning sunshine, I love you," while lifting off the block-out shutters, pulling back the curtains and walking over to him to tell him how proud I was of him. What followed was a feed a change of clothes and we proceeded with the very long day ahead.

In the early days of the routine, Ashton was on three sleeps between feeds and play. Each sleep, I would put him down at the exact time every day. It was monotonous and restricting, but created predictability which, in the long run, became the communication between myself, the mother, and Ashton, the baby. He thrived off it and it was beginning to work.

The day begun with his first nap being successful. I had two hours of cleaning the messy house, having a shower and getting ready for sleep. I had months of fatigue to catch up on, plus I'm pretty sure I was in some form of depression as I was still on survival mode. I still wasn't experiencing any joy, going out for coffee, a movie or dinner; that was the last thing I was thinking of. I was glad that I even found myself two hours in the day and night to sleep after four months.

The nap after lunch was a little worse. I would dread this time of day; my body even began to tremble around this time every day. No Egg Swing, car drive or baby carrier would work. It was so terrifying knowing that as the hours on the clock wound down, what I call the ratty hours, would begin and not subside until bath and bedtime. I would walk around the house feeling helpless, like such a failure and like a horrible human being not being able to soothe this little boy I cared deeply about. I would count down the hours until my husband came home, just wanting to see his face and not be in the house alone.

Matt has always worked long hours being self-employed, so seeing him come home at the same time every day was not a luxury I had. He did, however, do his best to get to us as soon as he could. Even then, I knew he had a long day, and I didn't want to dump a screaming baby into his arms as soon as he walked in the door. He was stressed out by all of this, and it had taken a toll on him as well. He had a business to run, and it wasn't like his weekends were free to take the baby out to have fun and explore. We couldn't take our baby out anywhere. He screamed more than he was content. Our weekends weren't like most others; they consisted of turning into silent pixies, eating for survival, working hard on reinforcing a predictable routine and catching up on much needed sleep when we could.

Every day was like this, and it was sending me into yet another dark spiral into a sad place as the situation of his reflux was still a massive issue that had not yet been solved. During this time, I was still trying to look for answers; the sleep I was now getting was helping me to think a little clearer and work from within. When you work internally, you start to make better choices. Acupuncture was the beginning of those better choices. I would take Ashton to acupuncture, and it's here where the doctor informed me that he had gut issues.

I told him about the afternoon screaming sessions and he informed me that it was because, at the end of the day, your stomach gasses build up and can be quite upsetting and unsettling for a baby. Although my body was beside itself with distress, I did manage to process the information and something in it felt right. This was the first health appointment that made sense and the first appointment that looked into how I was feeding my child and how I was feeding myself. Finally, someone looking outside the box.

Now, finally, we were onto something; a new path had been discovered and one I was willing to walk down.

The Not-So-Shocking Truth

Does one size fit all? Are 28 kids in a class all the same? Is there more than one way in doing anything?

So, why is there only one way to feed your baby?

Because it works for the majority.

Or

You must be doing something wrong.

No! I'm here to tell you that you are doing nothing wrong and it's ok to join me in the "minority" (or are we now the majority?).

There is more than one way to feed a baby; there are two that I know of and those are breast and bottle.

Which one is better? The one that works best for your baby and for you.

Another area where we as women have not yet managed is finding the emotional supportive balance, we need to supply each other. The stigma that one way is the only way, and the better way is still laying heavy in today's society and, for the life of me, I don't know why. It seems we haven't evolved with the times. To me, that evolution looks like supporting both sides and not segregating one from the other. It's about considering all the lifestyle factors that the mother is facing, like her work situation, her general and overall health, how much sleep she is getting, how much emotional and physical support she has access to, etc. Not everyone can give birth, leave a hospital and have the capability to create a healthy, full supply of breastmilk, despite what society will lead you to believe. For many women, this rings true, but for many, it also doesn't and it's my firm belief that there ought to be no shame in that. There are benefits to both ways of feeding not benefits to only one. I am an advocate of support feeding, not judgement feeding.

Why do I feel this way? In the early stages of Ashton's first year, when the screaming uncontrollably and crying all through the night and day would not surpass, the way I was feeding my little man was by breast. As you know, this is, of course, what the professionals recommend and I do believe that there is a lot of goodness in it, especially in the first few weeks. When I Googled the benefits of breastfeeding, this is what showed up: it's free, it increases your baby's resistance to infection and diseases, satisfies both hunger and thirst and meets their nutritional needs for the first six months.

Ok, that may be true, but also untrue for some. During my time of breastfeeding, I struggled to produce sufficient amounts of milk. I was so completely run down and stressed that my supply was either non-existent or on hold. This was from day one when the midwife had to syringe the colostrum out of me and, even then, she didn't get much at all. I was encouraged by all professionals to continue as I was told the baby latched well and drunk well. Not long after a feed Ashton would throw up acidic milk chunks and it would smell terrible. At times when he didn't latch well, he screamed and didn't want to go on; his little face was red, and he was sweaty. It was an unpleasant experience. It seemed I had more bad feeds than good ones. I continued to force him on and stick with it as I was always assured that this was the right way. I wanted to be a good girl and do the right thing; I was not strong enough to think for myself at that time. Gosh, it is bringing a tear to my eye just writing this. 'Nat what were you thinking? You really didn't listen to your gut intuition. Ah no, I don't have a gut intuition when I'm in flight or fight'. I gave all my power over to the nurses, websites and associations. I felt so disappointed in myself for listening to others even when it clearly wasn't working.

I'm sorry, Ashton, for putting you through that.

Before having the baby and while being pregnant, I never saw breastfeeding as gospel, or as the almighty way of doing things. I like the idea of it because it was natural, a way of bonding and I've always been a stickler for classic and traditional ways of doing most things. But what I liked compared to the reality of my situation when going through with it were two different things.

My birth plan was flexible; I had an idea of what I would like to do and that was to do it naturally and with no drugs. But I always had it in the back of my mind that if circumstances didn't pan out that way I would have hoped, then I would be open to the idea of doing what's best and safest for myself and the baby. Why is this not the same when it comes to feeding? Fortunately, my birth plan went according to what I had envisioned, and I gave birth naturally and drug-free. But I would like to stipulate that I don't think I am more superior or any more of a hero than someone that is brave enough to have a C-section. I applaud women for having the courage and self-love to ask for help in any form if they need it. I actually feel a little silly for not asking for some myself.

I am no stronger because I tolerated the pain. True strength is doing right by your heart and not meeting the picture that society creates. In the same way, I don't think you are any more of a hero if you breastfeed rather than bottle feed. In relation to my experience, the problem lay firstly in my insecure and vulnerable mental state and secondly in the one-sided world we are living in and the opinions of others. I was guided one way and it was not the right way for me. At that time in my life, I placed value on what others thought of me. I felt like I was failing at my motherly duty because my baby was always crying and unhappy; I chose to care about what other women thought. That's why I chose to breastfeed and kept trying to stick with it.

Eventually, sticking with it for all the wrong reasons had its day. I was brave enough to make the decision that I needed to look at this for what it was. Breastfeeding was not the right internal choice for myself and my son. My stress levels, my emotions, my hormones and my overall health, nutrition and immune system were at their lowest. They were completely depleted and at their worst. How anyone could recommend feeding a little innocent baby from such a deprived source is beyond me.

So, instead of taking on any more shame from society, I chose to make a decision that I figured was going to put my baby and myself in a better emotional, nutritional and healing position. That decision was to switch to a bottle and try formula feeding. I felt like the tins had more to offer than what I had. Bottle feeding would provide some sort of consistency as I could physically see how much our little guy was drinking. That alone provided a handful of answers, and answers are what I spent months searching for.

So, I was now bottle feeding and feeding with formula. How was our little baby? How was the experience? How was I, the mother? Absolutely, positively brilliant. By far, this was the best decision I had made when it came to being a mother. The first bottle he had, he drunk it like he had never had food before. He drank it right up. Little Ashton sat up, burped and then, nothing. It was silent. I was waiting for tears, for the arched back for spew up; nothing. He just sat there, content and settled. Hallelujah! Oh, and what came next was a huge, whopping sleep followed by a big smile and a happy boy.

There's that loosening of the chest. Ahhhhh, relief. Let's just sit in relief for a minute. Ahhhhhhhhhhhhh, Mumma's made a good choice. For a few moments, I remember feeling like "this is too good to be true". I cried and cried, but this time it was tears of joy; to be honest, I felt stupid that it took me so long to do this. Why did I spend so long persisting with something that wasn't working? I really overthought this. The bottle and formula feeding continued to be a success. I now received happy feeding times which snowballed into longer sleep times and resulted in a much happier baby boy.

In conclusion, the bottle was best for my baby and I. Switching to my truth and honouring what worked best for Ashton and myself was an act of self-love and self-belief. It took courage for me to make that decision in a world that supported the latter. Looking back, it showed me that even when I'm at my lowest and on survival mode and I think that I'm completely switched off on the inside, my willingness to keep getting back up and trying something until I find what the hell it is that will work is what ignites my soul, and my soul is there for me when I need it the most.

I want you to know that whatever you choose, if it honestly feels right for you and your baby, I wholeheartedly support you. My closet girlfriends breastfeed and some bottle feed; when we were together, it wasn't even a topic of conversation. They are not defined by the way they choose to feed their baby. They are not defined by the way they gave birth. The ones that breastfeed love it because it simply works for them and their child. So, too, are the mothers that bottle feed; they are happy because they are doing what is best for them and their baby.

Not Quite Out Of The Woods Yet

While I was elated that I had managed to solve a massive part of the puzzle, there was still some work left to do on finalising a great resolve to the whole unsettled gut related issues that had accumulated. Ashton was born with an inflamed gut, and I still had to work on cleaning up the months of irritation. I also wanted to know that I was feeding him the right formula. With my determined attitude, I was sure to find the last part of the puzzle that would enter Ashton into the world of a complete, content, settled stomach, permanently. Now that I was getting some sleep, my baby was more settled and content, and I was starting to feel my old self trying to shine through. I made the decision to change my direction on the health advice I was receiving from the local nurses and paediatricians as I had invested so much of the time and effort I barley had into them and never got far with their direction. So, I returned in the direction of integrative health yet again, and once again, I found all the answers I was looking for.

As my doctor at the time didn't see children, she kindly guided me to see one that did. When sitting down with this new doctor, she took the time to hear me out and was the first doctor that actually cared about my wellbeing, not just the baby's. She looked at me and said, "Natalie, you should have a baby in the bush." I looked at her strangely and she begun to explain what she employed by that. What she meant was that when you are out in the bush, you don't have all the outside opinions and influences of others. You have to rely on your own natural, motherly instincts; they are the best to rely on and will guide you to what you need to do and where you need to be.

I explained to her that I eventually got there, but my soul agreed. She took one look at Ashton and said it was his gut. Your gut controls your brain, and his gut was inflamed and run down and so was his immune system. She didn't once begrudge me for formula feeding; she said she could see that I had tried and done what was best. She than gave me probiotics to add to his formula, along with an immune powder and another gut powder. She also recommended that I switch to the most basic formula I could find—one that was as close to milk as possible and one that doesn't promote any of the unnecessary, synthetic add-ons like fish oils and added nutrients. We wanted to keep it as clean and simple as possible. Simple was best and we would add the recommended supplements Ashton specifically needed.

After not even two weeks of doing this, he was 100 percent better; no more reflux. It was a miracle, or a really good integrative doctor who thought outside the box, and a mother that never gave up. Even when I found this new approach, I still had to implement the health advice and keep Ashton on a routine. To say Matt and I were overwhelmed with relief was an understatement. I felt like, eleven months down the track, I could now step into motherhood. Now, I can go to playdates, attend swimming school, go to parks, enjoy kids' birthday parties. Life as a mother had just begun for me.

Fast-forward eight more years, I have had Ashton allergy tested due to an extensive amount of eczema on the back of his legs. After running the tests, we were finally able to identify exactly what it was that caused the flare-ups. Ashton was allergic to casein and whey—the two main proteins found in full cream milk. One particular practitioner asked me if I breastfeed. He then asked if I ate dairy and full cream milk while I was pregnant and while I was breastfeeding, which I replied with "yes". I said I thought I was doing the right thing, but he told me that in many cases, I was.

See, what you eat, your baby gets. Because I was consuming dairy all through the pregnancy and breastfeeding while consuming it, it was being transferred straight to Ashton to absorb and digest, and we now know his body doesn't tolerate it. I began to tell him that formula milk worked better. He told me that he could see how it would seem better and worked better but, ultimately, no cow's milk in any form would have. He told me that a stressed-out, depleted mother has no healthy supply and supported me as he felt it was the less of two evils to choose from at that point in time. Upon returning home after receiving these results, I immediately started to remove casein and whey out of all of our diets, not just Ashton's. Within weeks, his dramatic eczema was beginning to subside. After months, it was on its way out, and after a good year, it had disappeared. I finally found where the issue was—yet another relief. After all of these health issues, it is my conclusion that the problem is coming from somewhere; there's a leak and you just need the determination and mental stamina to find it. Whether it takes a day or a lifetime, there's an underlying issue and I just needed to get to the bottom of.

Colic, reflux and, to a smaller degree, eczema took me on a wild and mentally exhausting ride—one that I never want to jump on again. This ride has no doubt shaped me into the girl I am today. Never have I ever felt so hopeless and out of control. I still can't believe how I managed to survive. While going through it, the thought that "this is happening for a reason" would play out through my mind, over and over again. I would pray to my angels and beg them not to let this little boy suffer anymore, to show me a way out of this. My way out of this was my belief system; I had to believe in myself to get us out of it. It was the ultimate test of everything I thought I had come to previously. My beliefs guided me to the right help and the right way out.

Did it break me? No, it didn't. Did I feel like it did at the time? Yes. There were so many times I felt like I was a broken woman, shattered into tiny pieces. I had no hope left, no spirt left inside of me. Just when I thought there was nothing left, the fragments that remained of me would shatter even more until I was basically dust existing in a human form. This is how I felt for eleven months of my life. This is how I can sum up the fear I faced as I entered motherhood. This was my truthful experience, and I would be lying if I wrote it any other way. I was just trying to find self-belief, trying to find a way back to feeling whole again. I eventually got there. I would like to mention that there were some relationships that thrived knowing that I had turned to dust—those relationships are no longer in my life.

Through the moments of darkness, a voice, a feeling, a knowing would make its way to me. That thought was that one day, someday, my story would help someone else not feel so alone. This moment would be someone else's guidance, someone else's way out. By me going through it, I could be a voice to the isolating experience.

When your friends and family return to their own lives, and your husband leaves for work and no one else is there, when it's just you and a screaming baby that you can't seem to help, know that Natalie is with you. Natalie was here in this exact moment. I have been you, and my soul remembers and radiates love your way. I promise you; you are not alone and there is a light at the end of the tunnel, that I can assure you.

Round Two. I Made It Through the Final Round

How did I have the strength to possibly do it all again? The answer to that is that we left lot of time between pregnancies. I choose to heal myself both physically and mentally until I was over 110% back to my new, normal self. Matt and I got crystal clear about why we wanted to have another child and what we would do if we were faced with the same situation again, only this time, with a 4-year-old. We had to have a battle plan and think this one through. Ultimately, Matt had said that it was up to me as I would be the one spending most of the time raising the bub as he would continue with his businesses and offer support when he could. I was totally fine and ok with that.

The ultimate decider for me was coming to terms with the fact that it was a test between myself and fear. Unlike most times on my life's path, I was used to being matched up with self-doubt; but this time, it was fear. Fear of going through that whole experience again. I got caught up in what felt most dominant in my first pregnancy—a fearful experience, and one than didn't end for eleven months. When I choose to stop replaying the old story of how things panned out for me in the first pregnancy, I eventually concluded that I didn't want to become a victim to my old circumstances. I created a form of detachment from the experience. I realised it was something that happened in my journey, and it didn't define me as a person or a mother. It was then that I chose to see all that I previously went through with Ashton as one big life lesson that made me stronger for what may lay ahead. This was my time to believe in that strength. This detached mindset created a clean slate for me to begin a new path for my new pregnancy.

Besides, once I was out of the woods, I spent the next four years cleaning myself up and doing all that I could to return to myself, to the Natalie I spent the previous years before motherhood building. No effort goes unnoticed nor forgotten. Instead, this time, I returned with the life lessons that challenging year presented to me. Like always, I chose to grow stronger and wiser from the suffering. Nonetheless, I didn't want to return to it nor a screaming baby all while having another child to attend to. This thought was at the very back of my mind being told to behave.

At no point did I let it take over and consume me. The fear was present but never took up permanent residency for the duration of the pregnancy. Once the decision was made, fear had to take its place and it was my job to keep it in check. Let's face it, that's a job in itself; fear likes to creep its head in and out of situations, but I must admit, I did really well with not letting it. I even had a 4-year-old running around and worked part time, so I had my hands full. Fear was only a component if I was to let it be.

Baby Travis was born in the winter. I had exactly the same labour and birth experience that I had with Ashton. Travis was healthy and arrived safely. I am pleased to announce that Travis was not born with colic nor reflux; I never underwent any of what I went through with Ashton. Keeping fear in its place, not letting it consume me nor identify with me and make the conscious choice to move forward and detach myself from my previous experience I believe attributed to this wonderful result. Our minds are incredible magnets and, in many cases, can attract how we think and feel.

After giving birth, we got settled into our room with our new little baby, Travis. I felt good, and I say that because after giving birth, you are on a lot of adrenaline and your hormones are everywhere. I thought that this would be the time when the fear of four years ago of being in this room would come surging back to take advantage of the vulnerable state I was in.

Hours had passed, which turned into days, and our little Travis was settled, calm and content. No screaming, no vomiting; he just fed, burped and slept. Oh, this was amazing; what a miracle. I remember saying to Matt that even if we just get these few days and it all starts again, then I will still feel so grateful we had at least that; we have three more days than we did last time, we have three more days that we don't have to be living a screaming nightmare. Upon returning home, those magical days had been even more present; we were gifted with plenty more of them. This is what it's like to come home with a baby that doesn't have any underlying health issues. Wow, I could not have been more grateful for anything more. I'm so glad little Ashton didn't have to witness the heartache and struggle of a colic and reflux environment and the stresses it puts onto each family member.

After the first few weeks of having the privilege to settle in, I noticed Travis' feeds were not satisfying him. As all you mums know, if their feeds aren't good, then we start to have a snowball effect with sleep, unsettledness and play. The problem I had was that no matter how much I was feeding, it never seemed to be enough. I was advised that what was most likely happening was that Travis was cluster feeding, which meant he wanted a lot of short, small feeds more regularly and he may be having a growth spurt or just wanted more, so stick with it. As soon as I was informed of this information, it instantly didn't feel right; it felt like a band-aid over an open wound and a generic one indeed.

I am sorry to admit that I went against my internal beliefs for a moment and gave in to society and the majority yet again. I sat myself down on the couch and stayed there all day with the willingness to be there all night, too. As hours went by, I began to cry and cry some more; this didn't feel right. If Travis wasn't eating, he wasn't sleeping and as the time went on, he wasn't getting any more satisfied; he was becoming pissed off. I had to make a decision now – and fast before the exhaustion set in. I detached myself from the baby handed him to Matt and got some fresh air. As I stood outside, barefoot on the grass, looking into the sky, I took some deep breaths and tried to focus on my breathing.

Natalie, why are you doing this to yourself again? You've become unstuck, return to yourself and the answers will be in there. Trust yourself, believe in yourself, you know what to do, the problems are your doubting yourself. You're tired and drained but you've been through worse. This is your decision, and you know what's right. Step up and believe in yourself. Block out the noise; the answer isn't noisy—it's peaceful and uplifting.

Two words that fear and self-doubt removed.

I walked back inside, looked at my husband and my very tired and unsettled boy and made the decision to stop this nonsense; we were putting him on a bottle.

Second time around and, again, I slip into bottle shame by pushing myself to do what I was told was right instead of what felt right. At least, this time, I came to this realisation quickly and as soon as I did, I felt confident and proud that I did. Sometimes, just pulling yourself away and making the decision is harder than actually actioning it. If cluster feeding is what feels right to you and your child, I think, go for it, continue what makes you and your baby happy. That's what we are all striving for, right? If it is not, and anything doesn't feel right and results in a negative circumstance, then don't be ashamed and stop.

My personal conclusion is that cluster feeding is yet another example of the imbalanced support distributed between mother and baby, perhaps it's been there for years. The support the mother receives is minimal to none, guided to keep on keeping on, to stay awake all night, go without so you can give your baby everything and more. By all means, absolutely put your baby first in the majority of circumstances. I mean, we are the vessels, but we live in the 21st century and these vessels need nourishment, support, sleep, health and wellbeing check-ups. I can only wish to believe that we are moving into a society where the mother is seen as more than the servant and supplier. Yes, it is up to us to find the resources, but I can tell you that it can be difficult and challenging on little to no sleep and while raising a little human. All I would ask is to lift the load off the mother in today's society.

After birth, we can treat the mother as if she has had major surgery and needs the next six weeks to recover. Instead, we have a society where we birth humans and can be sipping coffee the following week at your local shopping mall (for some) and even those I don't believe have truly healed properly yet. We take nine months to nurture and nourish ourselves, have monthly and weekly scans, checks on our vitals to see how well we are doing and then once we have the baby, all that stops. How bout we have a nine-month check-up after the baby where we get not only the baby attended to but continue checking up on the mothers' vitals and, better yet, the mothers' emotional and mental wellbeing. I guarantee there would be a business just in that. Instead, we live in a society where "our mothers did it so you can, too." After a human has birthed a human, there is much to heal. We are never the same again and that's worth keeping an eye on.

So, finally, I had little Travis on formula; I took into account all the wonderful advice that I had previously learnt like choosing the most basic formula. I even added my own prescribed probiotics to it. Travis was so happy; he ate like he had never been fed before. I was happy and slightly disappointed in myself for not doing this earlier and slipping again. He slept like a log and when he woke up, he was happy and willing to engage in play.

Some of you may be thinking that it's just formula and it's just bottle feeding, that I'm overthinking. Perhaps, you are right. I'm glad there are those of you out there that have much more confidence in this area and to follow through with what feels right for you, can you please do me a favour and keep it up and spread the word to others? For those of you that may have fallen in my category, please use my situation as an example to step aside, take a deep breath and find your voice and your truth. Who cares what the world is doing? Your baby cares what you're doing, and he or she will soon tell you if they approve or not.

I guess I just slip a little in those early days—that first year. It seems to pull me into self-doubt, not as much as the first time, but it definitely does. I'm someone that thrives on sleep and rest—two resources you lack when having a baby. I admire the people who can cope better with a limited supply of them; I, for one, am not one of them. Sleep is the most powerful recharge for the constitution of Natalie. I just snowball into a grey mess without it. I'm still someone that enjoys a replenished daytime nap. Like all you mothers out there, we soon learn to function without it; we take what we can get, and we refuel when we can.

It blows me away that we are so heavily relied on for the survival of another human. We grow it, birth it, feed it and nourish it all while having to find the time and energy to keep yourself healthy, functioning and alive. How could any woman not feel empowered by this process? This is yet another example that we as women have nothing to prove to humanity. I admire the woman who realises this strength. It is these women who live in empowerment and know their worth. It is these women who don't use disempowerment or blame as weapons of self-destruction.

We become powerless when we feel the need to prove the truth of what already is.

The School Mum I Choose to Be

With a six-month-old by my side and a 5 ½-year-old ready to start school, life was about to offer me a new chapter. Welcome to life as a school mum. In many ways, I envisioned the day that my son would be old enough to spend a whole six hours on his own. Part of me thought he would stay a toddler forever, that he was born to stay a small child that relied on me for everything. But the sheer fact is that there comes a time when they have to grow up, become acquainted with independence and grow strength in realising that they have their own identity to discover. Most importantly, more than ever, I want my children to know that whatever identity they discovered within themselves, it belonged to them; they did not need to seek my approval nor become enmeshed with me.

The school life, in many ways, was as much a learning curve for me as it was for my children. Before entering on the very first day, I made myself a clear, nonnegotiable rule—this schooling life was about my boys and not about me. These next few years were Ashton's and Travis'; I wanted them to see that their mum was invested in them and that they were the number one priority.

I already had my time at school and had the opportunity to do what I wanted with that time. Firstly, I was not going to vicariously live through them, and secondly, as harsh as it sounds, I was not there to make friends and turn it into a social event in which things got bitchy, nasty and complicated. I had learnt my lessons when it came to female companionship; the majority did not have my best interest at heart. A lot of people operate through external appearance and material possession and I, for one, did not want to have a bar of it. So, being polite and offering my acquaintance at a distance was what I had to offer. I wanted to focus my time on my kids and truthfully, I didn't care how this looked—my true friends know who I am and, most importantly, I know who I am and what I have to offer. Unlike my schooling days, I was not going to give this out freely to have it taken advantage of; I learnt from my mistakes, and I learnt from my pain.

Sending your kids to school and becoming a school mum has often been referred to as a milder form of stepping back into high school. I have witnessed in a lot of ways how this statement can be true. Although I had my boundaries set in place, it didn't make me exempt from people pushing them and witnessing childlike schoolgirl behaviour. Ashton's first year of school exposed me to some of these areas.

While spending the first few weeks getting Ashton settled into his new class, I chose to walk him in and get him settled. This meant that I had to make sure Travis was fed a bottle then breakfast an hour later, which I would feed him in the car park as I was a stickler for set routine times. When it came to eating, sleeping and play, nothing and no one would break my routine that created stability in my life and bought me times in the day that I could get things done. Predictability was my companion. Of course, the routine changed as baby Travis grew months and months older.

Every morning, I would wake at 6:00 a.m. and, despite how I would feel (which was usually run down, and wishing for more sleep), I would choose an outfit, put my make up on and make my hair presentable. I was still a hairdresser and working part time in my salon so I chose to portray a presentable image as I may receive anyone of these people as clients in the future. And to be honest, I have always chosen to take as much pride in my appearance because I believe, at times, it reflects your emotional state. Admittedly, I didn't want people to see my emotional state, so I made every effort to hide it. I didn't want people to see me for the run-down woman that had lost a lot of her sparkle. I wanted to portray the girl that still existed on the inside but was bogged down with motherhood, diapers, baby food, kids' cartoons and baby playdates where we would talk more about motherhood.

So, I would get up, get myself dressed, make lunches, pack Ashton's bag, and when 7:00 a.m. hit, I would wake the boys up. This time was used to get them dressed, to bottle feed Travis, have Ashton's breakfast ready for him and get ready to pull up at the school. Then I would feed Travis his solid breakfast, pop him into the pram and walk him into school. Once Ashton was in class and settled, I would say goodbye and then rush home to put Travis down for his first daytime nap. Once this was done, I had an hour and a half to begin my housework, make phone calls and set myself up for the afternoon errands I needed to do. Everything had a timeframe and a schedule, and I juggled it all. Having a baby keeps you busy; having a toddler keeps you busy. Having kids is a fulltime job.

After the first term, Ashton begun bringing home homework and I remember thinking to myself that I didn't have time to sit there and do this with him. When I attempted it, Travis always demanded my attention. He was never going to sit still, be quite and just play. Nope, not my child. In my house, I was in high demand from the moment I woke up until the moment I went to sleep. After school finished at 3:10 p.m., a whole other routine began, which involved getting unpacked and settled, starting homework, dinner and keeping Travis entertained. My main priority, though, was to get the boys bathed and in bed, read to, snuggled and lights out by 7:00 p.m. I have never ever wavered on that bedtime routine. The positives always outweighed the pace at which I had to work to achieve it.

Besides, once my husband got home, I wanted to be there for him. It was very important to me to be a wife and a friend. Matt had had a long day at work and I'm sure he had challenges he had to deal with throughout his day, too. I wanted to be a place of happiness for him to come home to—not a stressed-out, run-down mother that resents her day and her life choices. Of course, once in a blue moon, I couldn't contain it because that's how I felt a lot of the time, but I worked particularly hard to pull myself out of it and focus on what I was grateful for and all that I already had. I found that really helped.

So, my everyday life was full; I couldn't possibly squeeze anything or anyone else into it. Actually, I could, but that would mean sacrificing one of my major priorities, like my children, the time with my husband or any time that I could squeeze out a tea break or a breather. Even if I found one minute to fill up my cup for the day, I would highlight that cup of tea in my daily gratitude practise and that would make me feel like I did something for myself, and that I wasn't just a slave.

As time went on, Travis' sleep times changed; he was on two naps a day and they were a little later, which meant that I was unable to go and do the school pickup as it would interfere with his sleep. Unfortunately, my children never had good transitions from car to cot. If they fell asleep in the car and the car turned off, that was it—there sleep time was done even if it was for ten minutes. I could get no more out of them. All you mothers know that makes for one crabby and long afternoon, counting down the hours until bedtime. Also, Ashton's school started having event days like Book Week, Mother's Day, The Letter P Day, sports carnivals, and end-of-year events. I was so used to day care centres where you drop them off and you pick them up. With school life, I was running back and forth, all the time. Something had to change; I couldn't juggle all of this anymore. I openly spoke to Matt about how I was feeling, and we both concluded that it was time we looked into hiring a nanny for some form of consistent help.

Hiring a nanny was a big step for me, but I did it and it worked out to be one of the best decisions I ever made. We chose a young woman that had the same characteristics as me. Her name was Madeline (Maddy for short), and she was amazing. Maddy was younger than me but had the same mind as me. We even look similar; when she would take Travis for walks, all the neighbours would wave thinking that it was me. I had never met anyone that had the same work ethic as I did, thought the same way that I did and valued my beliefs and morals the way she did. These were all the most perfect traits for entrusting your most prized possessions with.

Maddy worked five days a week for three hours in the afternoon. It was just enough time to pick Ashton up from school, come home, attend to Ashton's homework and prepare dinner. In this time, Maddy would stay while Travis was completing his afternoon nap; she would wake him, keep him occupied and feed him dinner then leave. She was my doppelgänger. I pretty much duplicated myself and split myself in two for the busy afternoon. By doing this, I pleased both boys, my husband and myself.

Maddy was incredible. She did her job like no other. I never once had to do her job for her; having help that didn't require me having to think for her and take the time to explain what I required was a godsent. She was always responsible, compassionate, reliable, honest and hardworking. Seeing her beautiful face and positive energy walk in every afternoon was the highlight of the one year I got to spend with her. Matt and I are forever grateful and hold Maddy dear to our hearts. To this day, both Maddy and her husband, Joel, have become dear friends to us.

So, with Maddy easing the afternoon pressure, I was able to get the other things done. It didn't mean that I had spare time to go and get my hair cut or catch up with a girlfriend; personal Natalie time was non-existent, unless you call tea breaks and eating lunch personal time (which I certainly do). Back in the baby Ashton days I was not so fortunate to receive those things and with Travis. I was, so I was counting my lucky stars. Like I said, anything over a screaming, unsettled baby is a win, and this time, I was winning.

I mention all of this to give you a brief understanding of what my daily life looked like when Ashton first started school. This was also why I was so reluctant to say "yes" to any social offers from the mothers. I was invited to many coffee dates, mothers' catchups, dinners out. I had so many invitations that I started to feel overwhelmed by them. It was flattering that I was invited, of course, but half of me just couldn't make it to any of those dates and the other half didn't want to get that involved because I knew where cliques and clique mums end up.

They were all nice woman, but when they are together and get to chatting and drinking, things sometimes can go pear-shaped. I didn't even have time for my own personal girlfriends; the poor things got put on the back burner because they understood where I was in my life. When I had a spare minute to myself, which was never, I wanted to spend that time with my husband or our friends, not a bunch of women that barely knew me—it just wasn't the right time. I chose to simply prioritise my time and stay focused on what was important and that was being the mother I wanted to be for my boys, the wife I wanted to be for my husband and trying my best to maintain enough Natalie to not lose myself to it all. It was a matter of simply realising that I can't and won't do it all. Each year, I will gain more normality and more Natalie; I just have to be patient and be in the process or run myself into the ground trying to wear all the hats. I learnt my limits; I've seen what limit-pushing can do and I don't want to end up that way.

Although I had my intentions, boundaries and priorities set, it was still hard to decline the offers that were presented to me. After all, I did like to please people and see them happy. Unfortunately, because I grew up that way and it led me down a path of shattering my identity and self-worth, I wasn't going to allow myself to do it all again.

Sometimes, choosing your wellbeing can initially seem like the harsh option, but I can assure you it's the option that will nourish your mental wellbeing and overflow into your family's. I'm a firm believer that your choices as a parent influence your children. How they see you deal with any circumstances, good or bad, are witnessed and adopted by your child. This may happen on a conscious or unconscious level. Even though my son was only five, I didn't want him to see his mother give in to obligation, or adult peer pressure and say "yes" to something she really didn't want to do. This was the energy around the situation and kids pick up on everything.

Eventually, Ashton settled beautifully into school, and I was still running around like a headless chicken, even with the help of Maddy. To be honest, the first year seemed like a car race being run at full throttle; rarely did I feel like I eased off the accelerator. I was always conscious of the fact that I was running at full speed, and it was not healthy, so I did what I could to stay in check. Every time I accomplished one thing, the school would send out another e-mail about another day or event to contribute to. "Your son has won the public speaking competition. He will be speaking at assembly on Monday at 9:30a.m." I would think to myself, 'Ah, that cuts into Travis's sleep. I will have to organise a babysitter. He can't come he doesn't sit still nor is he quiet, I won't be a moment present for Ashton if I bring him with.' Of course, it wasn't the school's fault they didn't fit into my tight-knit routine that made my world function. My children attend a beautiful school that I love and adore, and I am very grateful for all that it represents.

Ashton is currently in Year Five now and because I don't have a baby and I have myself sorted out, I enjoy all these events, especially, the yearly swimming and athletic carnivals as I loved them when I was in school. Even as I write these words, Travis is about to start Preparatory (first year of schooling). He is very excited and ready, as am I. I have dreamt of this day for so long; I couldn't picture little Travis and Ashton both going to school together. There are nearly seven hours a day when they're independent of me. It's their time to discover who they are without the influence of their parents.

What Goes On Behind The Juggling Act

Lord of all Lords, God of all gods hear me when I say the art of juggling parenthood, work life, and personal life is one of great magnitude. It is an art that is classed as a requirement here in the 21st century—one that we adhere to and one that we become accustomed to quickly.

Never in my life have I had to master an art so efficiently. Do I have it down pat? Yes, at times, and also, no. Just when you think you're on top of your circumstances, something else gets thrown in the mix where you're forced to press the refresh button, whether you like it or not.

On a day-to-day basis, I am blown away by the extraordinary effort that parents go through for their children. It seems we live in a world where both men and woman are playing the juggling act; I know my husband and myself certainly are. Becoming a school mother has shown me a whole new level of it. Some days, it blows me out of the water and other days I feel like I am the captain of the ship. I am a very organised and structured person, if you haven't already gathered that. I wouldn't say I have OCD (which there is absolutely nothing wrong with), but I like structure and predictability as this environment allows me to feel safe and comfortable to let go and give my all to my work and what is required of me. When I do anything, I like to do it with 110% commitment and dedication.

It's especially hard to do this when you have five areas, perhaps more, in one single day that need your attention, presence and time. Being this way has its pros and cons. I pride myself in quality of work and quality of person and I refuse to compromise on that. Therefore, spreading myself too thin, ticking all the boxes or having my kids be in every single extracurricular event is not an option. I am only one person, and I can only do so much before I fall into burnout, becoming angry and falling sick. Besides, we all have a different amount of item boxes available to us; some people have more than others. There are financial item boxes, but also physical and emotional item boxes. The physical help these item boxes contain help balance this juggling act and keep it under control or stop the juggling altogether.

The help may come in many forms like having a husband that finishes work early enough to pick up the kids a few days a week so you can continue to work. It may mean that you have parents you can drop the kids off to when you need a night out or someone to babysit for free. It may mean the grandparents can do school pick-ups or drop-offs, or they may be able to watch them on school holidays. The list could go on and on. Any form of help is help. If you didn't have to do it and someone is there with no hidden agenda or underlying conditions—they simply want to help their sibling or spend time with their grandkids, nieces or nephews or help a friend out—then that help is truly a wonderful gift.

When you have kids and you are a parent, let alone a working parent, help is forever in high demand, especially, when you have little ones. I do all the pick-ups and school drop-offs. While waiting in the pick-up line, I can't help but feel touched in my heart when I see the grandparents coming to collect their grandchildren. There is one couple that have been doing it since I had been at the school. You can see how much joy it brings to their faces. Not once in six years have I seen or felt in their body language that they resent what they do, that it is a hassle or that their kids "should be" doing it. I have often spoken briefly to them, and they take great pleasure in doing this—they do it so their daughter and son-in-law can work and give their grandkids a wonderful life. I see the parents there every now and then and they are equally as lovely. I see husbands picking the kids up in their work uniforms and I see lots of mothers to.

In the 21st century, women work, they go back as early as what feels right for them. Although this circumstance began way before the 21st century, it has become much more common for the father to play the role of the stay-at-home dad. To me this represents yet another example of the much more balanced demographic world we live in.

Matt is the main breadwinner in our household; I am grateful and very proud of him as he fulfills his role exceptionally. I also work part-time and I'm a fulltime mum to our boys. This is what we both decided on. For me, personally, being a part-time working mum is an absolute blessing. I find it less demanding as my fulltime mother job. That, of course, is no fault of our boys; they are not perfect, but they are wonderful children. I don't believe they could be any better kids for me to change my mind on the fact that motherhood is my most demanding job.

School holidays are quite blissful—it's school life I find takes the biggest toll on me. Again, that's not the school's fault as it is such a wonderful and supportive school. It's just life and the requirements I put on myself while they are at school. Juggling and balancing it all, that is what makes me feel overwhelmed.

When school starts back up, I have a set morning routine and afternoon routine I require (not expect) my boys to follow. That includes unpacking their lunchboxes, emptying their drink bottles, taking off their uniforms, unpacking their bags and putting them away. Night-time comes and they set up their swimming bags, basketball bags and any homework that is needed for the next day, lay their uniforms, etc.

Once the kids are in the car, I drop them off in the kiss-and-go line where you drive up to the school, they get their bags out, hats on, get a big hug and kiss and off they go.

This system is awesome, and I love it since I don't enjoy getting out of the car and engaging in small talk and gossip. I have never enjoyed small talk—it's shallow and external to me. I much rather arrange a coffee catch-up when I've made the time to get to know you and hear about who you are and what you stand for rather than the car you drive and what your husband does for work. The school pick-up and drop-off zones may as well be renamed the identity zones—the zones in which you wish to be identified by. These seem to be one of two things—the car you drive or the gym gear you wear or your lack of. It's a total crack-up and one that has me dumbfounded. Some people feel identified by the car they drive. It is like it represents where they are at in life and how much money they have. True for some, false for the majority.

I love gym wear, but I do not flaunt my body in skin-tight clothing that is so tight it looks sprayed on and a sports bra that just barely covers my nipples on school runs. It's good to see confident woman not hiding what they have but I personally don't see these women as confident; I see them as the complete opposite: insecure. My good friend is a school mum, and she is a weapon. Her body is insanely fantastic, she has four children, runs marathons, cycles with the best cycling teams around Australia, and works out all while running a household of the most beautiful children and husband. Rarely do I see her in gym wear that exposes her physique. She is not identified by her amazing body. Similarly, there are also plenty of mothers that are athletes at our school and at no point do they parade around being identified by the success of their bodies—I believe there is a time and place for that.

Another girlfriend of mine entered a body building bikini competition. Not only does she have an amazing body, but she is drop-dead gorgeous inside and out. When you meet her, the first thing you see is her obvious beauty, but once she opens her mouth and begins to speak, you will be blown away by her sense of humour and down-to-earth warmth she radiates. Besides the bikini competition, you would never see her parading around the local mall and school zones in next-to-nothing. Call me old-fashioned, but provocative wear and minimal clothing is for other places, not the two minutes of exposure you get from a school drop-off.

Your tits and car don't make you who you are.

I have tits and I have a car that I consider nice, but it absolutely does not represent who I am and how much money I have. My friends don't care what car I drive, and nobody cares about my chest size. I would hate to be known for these things; I am worth so much more. For the people that matter about external images, I steer complete clear of. You don't impress me. Again, there is a big difference between people that have a point to prove and those that don't. Generally speaking, people that have the money, self-confidence and value—the integral qualities of life—don't flaunt it and are identified by them. Now, there is nothing wrong with material possessions and having nice things; I just don't appreciate when people are identified by them as the first port of call. To me, it's like saying, "Hi, my name is Natalie. I own a Ferrari, what about you?" Ferrari or no Ferrari, I'm interested in what's under the hood (so to speak). So, pick-up and drop-off can prove to be an interesting time of the school day.

Once the boys are dropped off at school, I rush off to attend to my work. After work, I go back to pick up the boys and take them to swimming training or basketball training. Before Travis attended school, Ashton would take himself to these events and I wouldn't have to do pick up until later in the afternoon, which bought me so much more time in a day. These were the days Travis attended kindergarten and those hours are longer than school hours. Now that Travis has officially started "big school", I have one pick-up at 3:00 p.m. and another at 5:00 p.m. It sucks! There's so much waiting-around time and I have no item boxes I can use to help. This means that my work hours have to change so I can be available for my fulltime job of being a mother.

Ashton is a great swimmer, and he loves basketball. I believe sport is extremely important in a child's life. It has helped Ashton develop self-confidence and believe in himself. Also, it's exercise, so it's a great health benefit. My boys love to swim; Travis is still young and hasn't entered school competitions yet, but Ashton has, and he has represented his school for swimming, attends swim meets and trains in squad every other day. There are days when I drop off, rush to work, come back for after-school sports and run back home to make dinner all to have a 6:00 p.m. client waiting for me.

Some days, I feel like I am on fight-or-flight. When I notice this, I try to pull myself up on it, ASAP. Later that night, when my husband gets home and finishes his meal, I openly communicate how overwhelmed I feel and I begin to adjust areas that could work better for me, like scheduling my clients better or preparing a bigger meal the night before so dinner will already be prepared. Sometimes this approach feels like I'm writing lists on top of lists and spending all my spare time preparing for the uphill climb I have ahead of me the next day.

Sometimes, on a Sunday night, I feel like I've got a week-long marathon ahead of me for the following week. Especially when I know I have kids' birthday parties and weekend sports events scheduled in at the end of it. You see, us parents don't really get to go into the weekend with a free Saturday and a free Sunday. Saturdays are weekend sports followed by a birthday party or two. I sound like the world's most pessimistic mum, but when you've been your own item box all week, and you've done three jobs, the last thing you feel like doing is attending more events with loud, screaming kids and small talk. Granted, they don't happen every weekend, but there is usually something on. Yes, it is up to me to pencil in white space, and we do, but some weeks, there's just too many friends' parties, kids' parties and sporting events that are required of you.

Fridays are currently officially my day off, meaning that I get school lunches ready, take the boys to school head straight to the food shops and fill my cart with enough food to feed three hungry boys for a week. While there, I plan out my dinners in my head. Because I had forgotten to pick up the list, I took the little time I had to write from the bench. After that, I do my non-negotiable one-and-a-half-hour meditation with my weekly group of girls. It is my godsent and my absolute saviour. After that, I head straight to the shop to pick up a present for the party we are attending that weekend or run errands for school supplies, teachers' presents or pack for our vacation, so when I pick the boys up, the car is packed and ready to go. I basically have two whole hours to get everything done without the boys. Once 3:00 p.m. hits, I'm back off to school pick-up and afternoon sports.

Although this has changed every year as my youngest son has gotten older, I'll think I have it all sorted out and then it changes, and different requirements come into place. According to Eckhart Tolle, I have learnt to "watch the thinker". I have learnt to be aware when my mind has had enough and begin to see my ego creeping in and turning my mind into an unconscious place of self-pity and doubt. It's here where I begin to spiral into stress and see what and how much I have chosen to take on. It's then up to me to change my surroundings, even if I don't quite yet know how. The fact that I made the decision to take a step back and become conscious of my mind and thoughts has already put me in the right direction. I then begin to trust the process and make small but better choices. Before long, I find myself on top of the mountain and in order again. Yes, I get knocked down by the demands of motherhood and life, but by taking this approach and applying it, I never seem to get knocked down quite so far each time; I never fall as hard.

At the end of the day, it's up to me to be accountable for the situations I put myself in. With the recourses I have, I do my best. I don't have physical item boxes unless I choose to purchase them. In some cases, I do, but at the end of the day, it's a mathematical equation; things just have to add up financially. A business won't run successfully at a loss, and neither will I. I choose to organise and reorganise my time and spend our money on other areas where we as a family can enjoy and provide our kids with what we didn't have.

I commend all the people who graciously accept help. Why struggle? Why suffer? If someone is offering you help, free of conditions and expectations, receive it, friend. Kids don't need to be exposed to overwhelmed, burnt-out parents; it seeps through to them no matter how hard you try not to let it. We need to regroup, recharge and come back as the best parents we can be for our kids and for ourselves. Accepting help is an absolute sign of strength.

Parenting, Not For The Faint-Hearted. Do We Have A Choice? We Always Have A Choice!

From birth to baby, toddler to child, there is no doubting that the effort, commitment and dedication that is insured along the way to help raise these children is described as nothing more than gigantic. It's a mammoth task and a life-changing one at that. As I have mentioned before, you are just not the same person anymore. I even believe it to also be true when you adopt the role as a stepparent. When you are responsible for another life, you have much more to consider than just your own. For the conscious parents, it is yet another juggle to balance the requirements that are needed to fulfill your role while trying to still obtain some of the person you once were before becoming a parent.

There's no doubt that it's by far one of, if not the most rewarding job for those that wish to have children. It is also relevant to state that it is not the easiest by any means. I don't believe anyone sees parenthood as a walk in the park, despite how perfect your children are, which they aren't because, let's face it, no one's are. They wouldn't be having this human experience if they were.

Throughout the process of raising children, it's common for mothers and fathers to disconnect from their purpose and lose who they were. It's so easy to stay in the constant giving mode and settle into the demands of children and their life. I believe it's here where we need to be aware of the pull, of the complacency, and it's here where we need to ask ourselves, "Is this me? Does this situation light me up? Am I waking up looking forward to each day, or is it yet another day of survival?" For me, there was a major stage in my life where I was waking up for pure survival. I woke up to constant requirements; I felt pulled left, right and centre. I felt like my daily motherly inbox was constantly full with the needs and wants of the children.

To a lesser degree, the same applied to my husband. I simply can't believe how much some mothers do in a day. I felt like I turned into a mixture of Sadie the cleaning lady, old mother Hubbard, and a rundown, deflated woman. I often wished that I could swap roles with Matt for a day or two and be the main breadwinner. I would love to leave the house as a separate entity and have a change of scenery, a change of demands, meet new people, have different conversations—adult ones. There's only so many playdates in the same centres and parks you can visit and Nickelodeon you can take before it all becomes one big ball of a repetitious mum life.

I think it's fair to say that I didn't have any balance in my early days of motherhood. My life was mundane, repetitive and structured. That is what I needed it to become to be able to get a grip of the situation and the circumstance I had to deal with. I choose to give myself wholly to the experience, even if it didn't fulfill me every day and light me up. I chose this because it's how I could cope with the experience of motherhood. I did my best with the resources I had and the limited supply of item boxes. Keeping things simple and safe was how I felt I could control the many unexpected scenarios raising children can bring.

The first and early years of motherhood were really about survival. It was about staying conscious enough to hold onto the girl I knew I was on the inside. Even if I couldn't bring her out in my day, just reminding myself that she existed somewhere inside of me was enough to not completely lose myself and become someone I resented and someone that started to resent life.

Even on the darkest and heaviest of days, which was usually when I got sick and didn't have the physical time to recover, I had to dig deep, really deep, and find a way to somehow connect back to her. I knew deep down I was made for more than this life I was living. I knew I wanted part of this life, but not to the unbalanced extent I was receiving. Like everything else, it was up to me to pull myself out of it. Nothing would change if I wasn't to change it myself. But timing is everything, and no matter what attempts I made to ease the demanding motherhood, work-life balance I was in, the attempts kept sending me back down. Most days felt like I was trying to keep my head above water and try not to drown.

When lying in bed at night, when all the noise of the busy day was gone, I would listen to the sound of my breathing. It was in this moment that I would feel the urge to simply surrender. Intuitively, I was told to surrender to this moment in my life. My internal self wanted to, but my human body had resistance; it always felt like it could do more and give more. To my better judgement, I chose to listen this time. I was to let go, whether I wanted to or not. At no point did I see this as giving up—it was just letting go of the pressure I put on myself to get me into a more Natalie-fulfilling life, less of Natalie the mother and wife, the constant giver and non-receiver. I wanted to juggle the three beautifully, but I didn't seem to manage it. Motherhood liked to detach me from her.

I was doing two of them right, but my personal life was always falling short. But no matter what I believed that one day I would return, as my priority for never losing sight of Natalie was never compromised. My husband fell in love with her, I spent years finding love for her and when I reached that internal self-love, I never wanted to let it go. The more of her I can connect to and bring out in my day, the happier I am and the happier my three boys are. Each year, as the boys grew and became more capable and independent, I knew more of me would return, and that's exactly what happened.

I believe there's a difference between women who stay conscious of this slipping process and women who don't. I have been told hundreds of stories by women that feel guilty of missing and waiting for this part of them to return. I know of women who have forgotten that this awesome part of them even existed. It's so important to remember who you are, who you were before kids, who you and your partner were before kids. We had an identity before we were mothers and fathers; no one said we have to give up who we are and what lights us up in order to become parents. In fact, it's quite the opposite.

We all have purpose in this life. Each one of us is more capable than we give ourselves credit for. Some of us have been strayed so far off our path that we don't even know what that is, and that's ok. Don't be hard on yourself. I understand what it feels like to be in so deep you couldn't possibly imagine a life outside of motherhood—how could you possibly manage the kids and help them achieve everything they want. Not to mention be there for your husband, your best friend, and help him achieve all his hopes and dreams all while still having them all sit inside your heart, too. The big shocker is that accountability and consciousness will take you there, one step at a time. The process looks different for everyone and, yes, item boxes and cash injections will get you there much faster. But let me be proof that you can do it without them.

Aside from me surrendering to what was, I then decided to adopt a more physical approach to my morning routine. This would start by opening my eyes, turning my feet to the side of my bed, and placing them firmly on the ground. Once I did, I would begin by saying three things I am grateful for—one had to be about me personally.

- I'm grateful for my beautiful healthy boys.

- I'm grateful for my supportive husband.

- I'm grateful that I have managed to incorporate more plant-based food into both mine and my family's life.

Even if I didn't feel proud of myself for improving my family's nutrition, I would say it out loud anyway. Just hearing the words come out of my mouth was enough to eventually create a shift into all that I had and took me out of all that I was not and all that I was not yet achieving.

This small yet significant process helped pull me out of the uphill climb. It made me accept where I was even more and made me realise everything I already had. It took me out of the grey and placed me back into the colourful. When I was in colour mode, I attracted more colourful experiences, more colourful books, which led me to colourful podcasts, which opened my mind to a world of help that I could have never imagined possible. My thoughts and my actions began to resonate with the Natalie I so desperately wanted to reconnect with. I began to attend health and nutrition seminars, journal all that I learnt from podcasts—I replaced the radio for my weekly mind-upgrading podcast. I would study what I learnt and work hard at implementing it into my everyday life.

Even if all I could fit in was a cup of a new immune boosting herbal tea or adding some Ghee instead of butter to my cooking, I felt inspired by what I had learnt and proud of myself that I managed to add something healthy and nutritious into both my and my family's life. Something that may seem this small and insignificant to me felt like a great achievement. I would go to bed at night focusing on that experience instead of the pick-ups, school commitments, work and chores. In the morning when I woke, I would say how grateful I was to be living in a beautiful neighbourhood. I was grateful for a beautiful house and, finally, I was grateful that I knew how to cook healthy meals for my family.

I believe we are all performing hundreds of personal, purposeful moments in a day that we can be proud of that we can blow up to make them the positive focus of the day. Instead, many of us are wired to only see the negatives and we overlook the many amazing choices and actions that we make. Gratitude can be a fast way to highlight the magnificence that you are and be the shift into seeing all that you already have and all that you have achieved.

Gratitude was the shift from grey to colour. From the demanding life motherhood can bring to highlighting the parts of Natalie that always existed. I had now begun to live as a colourful mother. This process created the balance in motherhood I needed all along. I believe surrendering to what was, trusting timing and staying conscious of what I didn't want to lose comprised the recipe that created this beautiful place in motherhood that I'm in today.

Part 6

What Is In A Name?

There's a big difference between gaining a name or title through circumstance and earning the same name or title through your own actions.
Which will you be remembered by?

Heads up, there's no rainbow and unicorns in this section of the book. Life can get dark and ugly at times; it would be naïve to think otherwise. A massive part of my healing process was to discover that there are demons, villains and monsters that walk amongst us. They don't all exist within the pages of fairy tales; there are many walking around this very planet. And many of them are hidden inside of a significant name or title. Does this title/name give them the right to demonise us, to eradicate our identity, and destroy any form of internal self-love. Words can be used as weapons—verbal weapons, and they hurt. It's here in this part of the book where I have created what I like to call The Verbal Dictionary of Weapons as a place you can come to reference what they really mean, as opposed to what you are being called under reactive circumstances. Nobody holds a big enough name to subject you to verbal, emotional or any forms of abuse.

It is very important for me to share this part of my voice with you, with every intention of helping you find freedom in yours. To help get me to that place of freedom, I first needed to better understand the many tactics that were being played out in front of me, the many words that were thrown at me and the many different types of conditioned environments I had continued to keep myself in. It was only later in my life I found an extensive team of professional healers that guided me along the way, I never had one specific place to reference these ugly words (hence, this part of the book). There was the dictionary, of course, and I could dig through all my many self-help books. But here, in mine, I wanted a space for you to not only reference the ugly stuff but to read a personal example of my association with it. By doing this, I hope to provide you comfort in knowing that you are not alone in your pain. I have felt the weight and the agony of what I call Verbal Weapons, because that's exactly what they are—weapons.

Verbal Weapons are designed to destroy any form of self-belief and love for oneself—missiles built to aim straight into the heart where true impact can be established, and the foundation of trauma can begin to spread like wildfire. Verbal abuse is real; emotional abuse is real, and the weapons used to create the war are words. These words don't always come from insignificant situations. Usually, they come from significant people that play a massive role in our lives. What I put up with because of who they are and the name they hold is something that I needed to personally address. My mind, body and soul had been at war for too long, fighting battles I never stood a chance at succeeding. I never wanted to go to emotional war, but sometimes we find ourselves in situations we can't seem to find a way out of, no matter how hard we try. Sometimes, it feels like we can never truly escape the war because of the name that holds us to it.

Name
Noun

1. A word or set of words by which a person or thing is known, addressed, or referred to.

Becoming a mother and wearing the new name of 'Mum' was something that I became accustomed to quickly. It was a new title I was unofficially given when I birthed my children into this life. "Mum" was the name I was going to be called for the rest of my life; what an honour it is to be able to wear such a title. Like many of us, I, too, go by more than one name and have more than one title. I am a mother, wife, daughter, sister, daughter-in-law, friend, hairdresser, author speaker and, equally important, a Natalie (a soul having an individual, human experience).

The reason for this chapter is to clearly stipulate that no matter what name I am called or what title I hold, it's the meaning and the value I give to those names that ultimately create the true significance of it. The question I ask is, at the end of the day, do we want to be remembered by the letters that construct a name or do we want to be remembered by the person we chose to be behind those letters, behind the title?

After all, there are millions of Natalies, millions of mothers, millions of daughters and wives. Therefore, it is up to me, to us, to create an individual meaning and offer value, not only for ourselves but for those who we cherish and hold dear to us. We do this by realising that what we do, say, think and feel create actions which create memories and it forms an individual identity (a meaning). That meaning, those actions, the people we choose to become, and our choices are what separates us from all the others that hold the same title as us. Our actions, our intentions and our true hearts' desires are what's seen and what leaves an ever-lasting mark on this Earth and on the people we meet and love.

This topic of what's in a name is something I am truly passionate about. I feel it's such a taboo topic that not many have the courage to speak up about for the sheer fact of being called disrespectful, which is a name in itself. There are two types of people in this life—people that work hard on being that significant meaning behind the name and people that see that the meaning is irrelevant because the names of mother, father, husband, best friend, etc. are simply enough. Their name places them on a different platform and on a different level, which we all know creates separation and disconnect—two key ingredients for an unsuccessful relationship where constant expectations are birthed, and the word 'should' gets thrown around.

These people see that the title holds more value than the meaning. On the contrary, there are people running on investing time, love, support, adding worth, doing the constant hard work of maintaining the relationship and playing their part in their role or title—being seen as more of who they are not necessarily by what they are called.

It is here where I begin to open you up to a world that some of you may know of—a world that was created by a name that brings with it so much controversy, so much anguish, so much suffering, yet, in some cases, can provide the complete opposite. This name was the most common topic brought to my salon chair throughout the past 20 years, with nearly everyone sitting down and wanting to openly express the pain they were going through, knowing fully well that they could not speak up about this taboo topic to those that wore the name. That name I'm talking about is family; we all have them, but we all have different experiences with them. I have grown up in a world where value is placed by the name you hold and the rank in which you hold it in—a place where they have the sheer right to treat you any way they wish because the name holds such authority and gives them a get out of jail free card.

For years, I have grown up feeling the utter imbalance of the family hierarchy. I am not a girl that cares about coming last or being at the bottom; competition is not something I feel comfortable with. I have no issues letting someone go first or handing something over in order for them to feel worthy. My point being that, just because I am sitting down the bottom or below someone, doesn't mean I can't, or we can't, still be heard, loved and cared for. For as long as I can remember, my voice was being devalued because of my name as daughter. Hierarchy was significantly valued and the lower you were to the bottom of that hierarchy, and the louder your voice was (or just having a voice), caused much harm and condemned you to being classed as a disrespectful girl.

In the family hierarchy, the names higher than you gave you the right to treat people however you see fit; having the name of mother or father gave you every right to access emotional abuse, condition people into a system that served only you, the right to pour an overload of expectations onto another and devalue any worth you fought to keep. They continued to keep alive and thriving the hierarchy that had been previously working for years, knowing fully well, deep in their own hearts, that they, too, are trapped by it and wish to get out of it but are not brave enough to do so. Instead, they project what never served them onto another new generation because it's what they know and accept, and what you are expected to accept. This is generational trauma at its finest, and I struggled a lot of my life to break free of it. I was scared to put a voice to it because I did not want to be seen as a disrespectful girl and looked at with disgust. I also did not want to be subjected to isolation and ostracised for not accepting the hierarchical form of emotional abuse, which is what I had been so very accustomed to.

But it is here in these pages that I openly write and let the fear of being called a name not hold me back any longer. I want to let everyone who is reading the pages in this book know that just because they have the name of family, it does not give them the right to treat you untoward. It does not give them the right to disempower the person you are because you don't meet the expectations they demand of you. Don't allow anyone to treat you like shit and say, "I am your mother," or "I am you father," or "I am your husband," or "I am your best friend," and complete it with, "I love you." No one wears a big enough name to condemn you. Only you can believe them and condemn yourself, which is what I have learnt. A name holds no power if that name isn't operating from a place of unconditional love.

What we put up with because of who others are is on us. The hard truth and what I spent years denying is that there are simply functional families and dysfunctional families; there are functional relationships, be it friendships or work environments, and there are dysfunctional ones. I spent years taking responsibility for people that took none. In return, it just left me sick and began destroying anything good I had created in my life. My soul would cry out for love, worth and to be valued, all while I gave those things to people that withdrew them from me. I didn't listen to my gut intuition because I didn't believe I had the right to do so. Anything I had and all that I was I handed over to people that held a significant name. In return, I was told I was loved and, under several circumstances, treated differently. Their actions never matched their words and that's why I lay dormant and confused.

There are people who take advantage of their status and use it to disempower you and build their sense of self. Family is no exception, but many of us do accept the emotional abuse the anguish because they are exactly that—family. Family—a name that we all associate with individually and differently. Every family is different; no family is the same. My children will have their own personal meaning of what family means, and they will have my actions to go by. "Everybody is doing their best" is a statement I hear from many self-help books, and I couldn't disagree more. Yes, a lot of people are doing their best and are succeeding at it, but a lot of people are also lazy, victims of their circumstances, stubborn or rely on the status of their name to pull them through and bear the majority of the weight.

There is no luck involved in the thriving, functional, unconditionally loving families. The dynamic and demographic built to continually hold such a thriving environment is monumental and to be purely treasured like a precious jewel.

When I think of powerful meaning in a name, my heart takes me straight to the ever-beautiful Princess Diana. She was kind, she was pure; she left a legacy of compassion and love, and she will forever be remembered for the magnificent soul she was and the ever more significant impact she left on this world. Her name will be remembered by her actions, and by her intentions. To me, Princess Diana is the perfect example of the meaning behind the name. She was so much more than her title; she lived true to herself and honoured her integrity.

When I think of unconditional love, I think of Princess Diana and the way she looked at her children and the children of the world. When I think of a mother's love, I think of Princess Diana and how pure and selfless she was. To see a mother surrender her whole heart to her children and want nothing in return simply set a standard in my mind of what I would aspire to be towards my own children. To give her children the foundation to have felt so unconditionally loved in what I can only imagine would be quite a conditioned environment, is such a phenomenal feat.

Personally, I believed she worked hard every day to attain a beautiful bond between herself and her children. She never once seemed to be the sort of person to walk around entitled or, for that matter, titled. She is remembered by the way she made people feel and the presents she bestowed; it was more priceless than any title.

My wish is for my boys to feel so unconditionally loved that, no matter what happens in life, they will always have a place deep in their heart that they can return to and access an endless supply of it. I want them to know how I feel about them through my actions. I would like them to remember me by how I made them feel, and how I contributed to not only their life, but life in general.

I see leaving a legacy as hard work that I need to attain each day. I would very much dislike being remembered purely on the name I was given the day I birthed my children. A lot of people can be given the opportunity to be called "Mum" but how many give the name "Mother" a meaning? I don't wish to be remembered because of my motherly duties; I wish to be remembered by the continued effort, the constant support, the unconditional love that I action, and continue to action, until it's my time to leave this Earth.

"They won't remember me by name, but for the way I made them feel."

Natalie Falicz

When that time comes, my boys may be saddened by the physical loss. However, if I've done my job to my full extent, they will feel an everlasting, eternal presence that lives within their hearts that will forever comfort them and never be lost. Every day, I can create meaning and give meaning—to live with honour and live with integrity, letting my actions express volumes to the words I speak.

Below, I have listed examples, words, that have been a part of my healing journey—words that were intended to throw me off my path but, fortunately, I chose to take what was designed to break me and see them for what they really were—one major lesson. I learnt the meaning to all these words as I believe knowledge is power. It was especially important for me to highlight these words and announce their true definition and therefore give you a small insight to my experience and thoughts underneath them. I wanted to find these words a place in this book—an area for you to open up and reference them, as ugly as is it may be, to know that such things, such words, such names, exist. I, unfortunately, was completely naïve to some of them, and it was not until very later in life, through many forms of healing and therapy, I discovered such words exist and that there really are names for the different types of being mistreated. As soon as I gained knowledge and understood such meanings, it gave me a much better insight into how the unconscious, conditioned mind works, no matter what name it held.

We have always had the choice to stay and accept it, or to remove ourselves from it. The choice is always ours. You matter, your worth matters, your happiness matters, and you do not need to feel guilty or ashamed for wanting goodness and love for you, even if you do not 100% understand what that looks like or how that feels.

Verbal Wepons And My Personal Association

Respect
Noun

1. A feeling of deep admiration for someone or something elicited by their abilities, qualities or achievement.

2. Due regard for the feelings, wishes, or rights of others.

It is my personal belief that we can be taught how to show respect and be a respectful person, but it cannot be demanded of us. Respect is an authentic feeling; in relationships, you can't fake deep admiration and a high regard for someone—it has to be felt and earned. The problem is that the inauthentic demand it. I couldn't possibly imagine demanding my sons to feel a certain way about me and to treat me in an ideal way that suits my liking just because of the name I hold. Nor do I want them to match some past centuries' idea of what respect looks like.

I certainly don't require them to treat me in an idea of how sons should treat their mother. That is a huge expectation and an unforgivable entitlement that I do not believe in my heart is a good foundation for any loving relationship. Holding such an entitled and superior belief of oneself would only lead to the crash, burn and demise of any loving relationship. How can anybody rise to someone else's self-envisioned belief system? If there is no rule book on how to raise kids, there is also no rule book on how a mother should be treated, or a father, a son, a daughter, a sister, a brother, for that matter. Every family is different; every person is different. Every love is unique to each relationship. So, why is respect expected to look a certain way?

Mutual respect in any form of loving relationship is a two-way street, no matter what age—infant to senior. It is here, in the 21st century, where I am fortunate to witness many loving successful relationships that have evolved with the times. These relationships bring with them an equality and a generous balance of mutual admiration and respect for one another, no matter the name, title and status that they hold. It's these conscious humans that have thriving, enriched relationships—ones that support the mental wellbeing and growth of the individual identities.

Relying solely on the name you are given, the title you receive is nothing more than a shallow and superior way of thinking; not to mention an outdated one at that. Surely, you are more than a name. Surely, you go deeper than the letters constructed together. A name is powerless until we give power to it. Our actions, our intentions, give it meaning; the love we hold for ourselves inside the name is what reflects back at us. For it is the people that hold themselves in little regard that have to demand a feeling that has not yet been felt by them themselves. That has not yet been earned within them themselves. Loving admiration and high regard are earned through being an example of exactly what you're asking for.

Disrespect
Noun

1. To lack special regard or respect for someone.

Having a voice, speaking your truth and finding the courage to stand up to what doesn't feel right, is not disrespectful.

Discovering your worth, creating personal boundaries to protect yourself emotionally or physically is not a sign of disrespect.

Living in the 21st century, navigating your way through life, doing things differently than those that came before you are not a sign of disrespect.

Speaking up and openly communicating your true feelings from a place of pure intent, honesty and love is a form of love in itself; I believe one may describe it as self-love. It takes unshakable strength to find your voice and use it in an environment that has been conditioned to believe that speaking up is a sign of disrespect.

This inhumane concept has brought centuries and lifetimes of people being shamed into silence and conditioned into hierarchical systems that serves only a form of control—control over others, control over the majority.

Know, you can't command someone to hold you in a special regard; you have to actually be that special, put in the work and act from a pure, unintentional heart and not want anything in return. Special regard is earned; it's not in a name unless that name earned the meaning.

Respect is earned; it does not automatically reside in letters that form a name. Respect is mutual, not one-sided.

Hierarchy
Noun

1. A system in which members of an organization or society are ranked according to relevant status or authority.

2. A group of people or things arranged in order of rank.

Family Hierarchy

1. Refers to the structure in which the parents possess greater power and authority than their children.

2. The desired and necessary structure of a family.

Do I believe there is a place, or perhaps places, where a form of hierarchy can be beneficial? Yes, I do. Do I believe a family environment or any relationship where love is involved is one of them? No, I don't at all.

How can the placement of "I am above you" or "You are below me" be healthy for any loving relationship? I have already mentioned previously what putting someone on a pedestal can do—it creates a platform of separation. Whether someone else sees themselves as above you, or you see yourself as above or below someone else, it only creates disconnection. Nothing is mutual when there are people placed above and below you.

In a family hierarchy, you have to give up all of who you are in order to be the version others create for you—the version that is acceptable to represent their image; an image that would overlook how they treat you on the inside and will filter a false image on the outside.

Does that mean the person "above you" holds more power? What is power? To have control over others? No, that's called fear, and like any feeling, fear-enforced power is an illusion. To me, the true definition of power is unconditional love— not conditioned love.

Unconditional love requires no form of hierarchy; it is a powerful force that flows equally throughout the family, where mutual admiration is extracted from each individual member. As each member is seen, heard and valued for their individual self, thus creating a strong team known as a functional, loving family unit.

I have had the pleasure of being a part of some beautiful examples of families that operate in this exact way. This is especially important in this modern age where we are trying to bring forth more equality and be examples of voices being heard and people being seen for who they are, not what they are conditioned to be.

Conditioned

Verb

1. Have a significant influence on or determine the manner or outcome of something.

In a loving relationship of any kind, conditioning someone to be what you want them to be, or worse, need them to be, is a form of emotional abuse. It is a form of control, and when you need to control someone, you are simply powerless (lack of love in your life). People that feel unconditionally loved don't feel the need to control others.

Toxic people condition you to believe the problem isn't the abuse itself, but instead, your reaction to their abuse. – Anonymous

Unconditional Love

1. Unconditional love is known as affection without any limitations, or love without conditions.

2. Simply put, love without strings attached. It's love you offer freely. You don't base it on what someone

does for you in return. You simply love them and want nothing more than their happiness.

In the book called, The 5 Love Languages of Children, by Gary Chapman and Ross Campbell, Gary describes unconditional Love as "a full love that accepts and affirms a child for who he or she is, not for what he or she does." Gary continues to write, "conditioned love is based on performance and is often associated with training and teaching techniques that offer gifts, rewards, and privileges to children who behaved or performed in desired ways."

Gary then states, which I find significant, "Of course, it is important to train and discipline our children, but only after their emotional tanks have been filled."

This resonated so deeply with my soul. Not only does it apply to children but is also completely relevant to adults. I would like to shed light on the fact that there are adults that have been brought up with empty emotional tanks, never being seen as enough, always being demanded more from. Grown adults, accepting relationships where they are still being trained and disciplined to perform and behave in a manner that servers the hierarchy.

This is not love, this is not freedom; this is service and to serve on an empty tank can be detrimental to your emotional health.

Expectation
Noun

1. A strong belief that something will happen or be the case.

2. An expectation is a belief about what might happen in the future. It can also describe something that is supposed to happen.

It is my foundational belief that expectations are the number one destroyer of all relationships. Any accountable person does not live with expectations. I do not; I've learnt many years ago to replace expectations with requirements—that way, I can own what I say and stand in my truth.

Requirement

Noun

1. A thing that is needed or wanted.

2. A thing that is necessary or compulsory.

Can you see the big differences between the meanings behind the words? One is accountable, strong and clear—like setting boundaries. The other uses grey area words like "might" and "supposed to"—there is a sense of entitlement just in that word. Nothing is clear about "might" or the word "belief"—we all have different beliefs; everyone has different beliefs about nearly everything. Expectations are unclear guidelines created by people that demand more than they give. How can you have a relationship of any kind with unclear guidelines? When we are honest with ourselves and we actually say, out loud, what we really want, what we really require, we will see who we really are and how much we ask of others.

Expectations have nothing to do with another person and everything to do with the individual self.

It takes a strong person standing in their own power to speak up about what they truly want. It's not easy; that's why so many don't do it. It's much easier to take the powerless road and expect someone to just have read your mind or "should just automatically have known."

The thing is, nobody owes you anything! Nobody owes us anything! Nobody owes me anything! I am not entitled nor am I privy to anything I do not earn or bestow upon another. I am merely a reflection of what I give and if I give my heart and I am met with a sword, then I know it's not my place to reside. I do not ask the sword to become a heart for I have accepted the sword for what it is, not what I need it be, nor what I want it to be. What's more, I don't place a passive expectation on the sword to endeavour to be something it cannot be—for that is slowly killing of the spirit and the true value and purpose the sword was intended for. Everything and everyone has a place and a spot in life.

Becoming attached to a certain outcome from another person is extremely dangerous, and simply unfair. I don't know how anyone can have a relationship with someone's expectations—it's doomed from the start.

I expect you to be this type of friend.

You should be this type of daughter.

I just thought you would be this type of sister.

I just thought you would be this type of husband.

If you were honest and took ownership of your words and your demands, you would see that what you were really saying is I want, I need, and these are requirements.

Expectations are unaccountable requirements.

Accountability
Noun

1. The fact or condition of being accountable; responsibility.

2. An obligation or willingness to accept responsibility or to account for one's actions.

I believe you have read this book for long enough to know that this is my all-time favourite word. For me, accountability is the word of all words. If I could discover a formula for accountability, I would mass-produce it and sell it in tiny bottles. I believe it is the antidote that would make humanity look completely different. I believe it is the antidote that would keep relationships thriving. I believe it will equally kill off anything inauthentic as nothing inauthentic can survive in an accountable relationship and environment.

I wake each day making sure I take ownership of all of my actions, and all my words. I place strong value in teaching my boys to take responsibility in every choice they make—even if they find themselves not at fault, they are to find reason in how they would have ended up involved in that situation or circumstance.

Unaccountable
Adjective

1. A person, organization, or institution not required or expected to justify actions or decisions; not responsible for results or consequences.

Simply put, a callous and cold-hearted and irresponsible way to live a human life; it's no way to live a life of any sort.

One may argue that those that live unaccountably and take no responsibility for their words and action aren't living a life at all. For they are merely switched off, unplugged from the beautiful riches of life and instead reside in the unconscious mind where no ownership belongs, using projection as a tactic to throw onto others what they are not willing to look at and be responsible for. I used to believe that it was my job to take on that projection because the person projecting their unhealed, unacknowledged trauma held a significant name and told me they loved me. Dealing with what they projected unto me showed that they felt loved and cared for. When they felt this way, it earned me brownie points; and when all the brownie points added up, it would buy me love and acceptance and the freedom to be Natalie for just a bit. I enabled the behaviour because I didn't believe I had a right to believe anything more for myself. I put my worth in the hands of a name and into a narrative that was completely false.

We all make mistakes—it's part of life; we all act out-of-character and say and do things we wish we hadn't. We are here to learn and grow and, from what I have learnt so far, part of that process is learning where I played a part in making that mistake and being accountable for it. It doesn't end there—that's a start, but it's about researching ways, learning ways, for me not to make the same mistake again and being honest when I use the word "sorry". Am I sorry or am I just saying it to smooth things over and sweep it under a rug for a band-aid fix? I only use the word "sorry" when I wholeheartedly feel it and want to do everything in my power to change what I did wrong. I use "sorry" when I feel deep remorse and really want to be a better version for myself and for the person or people involved. I've heard the word "sorry" thrown around like it's a basketball; rarely do people add weight or empathy to the word. A heartfelt, genuine apology heals the situation; just speaking the word is not enough. It's just letters formed together to create a word that we understand—what's inside the word and the action behind the word, is what counts.

My actions speak louder than my words; my intentions speak louder than my voice ever will.

If I can't physically and emotionally show someone that I'm sorry, then I do not class it as a "sorry".

Unaccountable people use it in their vocabulary but don't associate with the meaning of it, which is a form of manipulation in itself.

Questions I've asked myself before are: How do you have a relationship with someone that refuses to take any form of responsibility? How do you have a relationship with someone that has preconceived ideas on how that relationship should look?

Do you spend your whole life trying to match that idea because of their name, their title?

Do you simply accept being treated in a way you would never choose to be by another just because of who they are, or how high they are ranked?

When it came to friendships or choosing a boyfriend, I found it easy to simply not put myself in those conditioned environments. I wanted to be in relationships where I was valued for all that I am and appreciated for all that I had to give. I would never be with a guy that didn't value my worth and took advantage of my soul. When I was in charge of choosing who I could have in my life, I wasn't going to choose people that conditioned me into a version that they needed me to be.

So, why are we required to accept this kind of behaviour from those that carry a higher name than us, or from the environments we have been birthed into?

Perhaps, it has been instilled in us that this is simply the way, the one way, the only way. So, you are programmed to believe that you must obey or be condemned.

Condemned
Adjective

1. Condemned to a particular punishment, especially death.

2. To declare to be reprehensible, wrong, or evil.

Condemnation
Noun

1. The act of saying that something or someone is very bad and unacceptable.

I have experienced condemnation in this lifetime. It is honestly heartbreaking. For me, it was the largest knock to the ground and the heaviest emotional punch to recover from. In many ways, it's the driving force to speak my truth and write this book.

I gave all of myself, continuously, for as long as I could, doing exactly what I was told from hierarchy, not putting a foot out of line. Anything I could physically and emotionally give, I gave. Even when it wore me down and it would put me into a state of fear (like panic attacks and ending up in the hospital), I would continue to keep giving all of myself to those that expected it from me.

After extreme exhaustion and connecting to a state of depression, I began to turn the volume up slightly on my voice. Although low, I spoke up about how I was being treated, how I was not being heard and how I wanted to be appreciated and valued for, at least, part of what I was giving. Sometimes, this approach would buy me a couple of months, perhaps half a year, but no matter what, I would always find myself back in the same position of not being or doing enough. As time went on, and as I grew older, the volume of my voice grew louder. Once, I even had an outburst at way too high a volume as I thought that by just letting it rip, I would finally be heard. It wasn't the right thing to do as I had learned the right and wrong ways to handle the situations I had always found myself in.

I tried finding where I could continuously be accountable in any situation as that seemed to soften the blow; I would be able to be heard more if I showed that, somehow, the situation was my fault. It wasn't until years later that I realised being accountable for yourself is one thing, but to take accountability for others' wrongdoings was not only wrong and untruthful but created a platform of requirement that was expected of me whenever a situation arose. To your not-so-surprise, I wasn't the only one in the wrong all the time—even though I was expected to carry that shame because of the title of the name and the hierarchy involved.

To be condemned for speaking your truth in a kind and civil manner and with sincere intentions is isolating. To be condemned for realising your self-worth and speaking up about not tolerating anymore forms of emotional abuse is unimaginably heartbreaking. To be condemned for setting healthy boundaries to protect and preserve your emotional health is soul-destroying, to say the least. To be condemned by people that tell you that they love you is extremely puzzling and manipulative.

Manipulation
Noun

1. The skilful handling, controlling or using of someone.

2. A manipulative person knows how to twist words, play on emotions and otherwise manage a situation in a sneaky fashion to get what they want.

Gaslight
Verb

1. To manipulate someone by psychological means into doubting their own sanity.

2. It is the act of manipulating a person by forcing them to question their own thoughts, memories and events occurring around them.

3. Gaslighting is a tactic in which a person, in order to gain more power, makes a victim question their own reality. It's done slowly so the victim doesn't realise how much they have been brainwashed, nor does anyone else around them suspect.

In a field of lions, nobody suspects the snake. Nobody is watching the passive slither of the long and venomous serpent. The lion may make too much noise; they stomp, they roar and if you were physically hit by one of them it would be loud and obvious. Is anybody watching the silent entrance of the snake? With one simple bite, it can send enough poison through the blood of the fiercest creatures to slowly, over time, end their life. The bite may or may not be visible, but the internal effects that come after are. But which one, I ask, do you fear most? Which creature is most deadly? Which approach is most deadly—the one that is obvious or the one that is silent and understated?

I have learnt to look for the snake.

When the snake has done its damage, it slithers away, nowhere to be seen; nowhere to be punished, nowhere to be accountable. It simply slides back into its life, never to learn its lesson. Gone are the days where humanity acts like obvious lions. If we are seen for our toxicity, then we will be forced to be held accountable. It's much easier to submissively inject our poison into someone's life and then run away and hide behind a false narrative, making the lion question their own reality of what actually happened.

Lions are known to be aggressive, assertive and demanding; they're loud and they speak up. When something is bothering a lion, you are sure to hear about it. What's wrong with that? At least you know where you stand with a lion; you have somewhere to work from. It's easier to pin it on the loudest person in the room, or the one that was courageous enough to speak up. It's also extremely cowardly when you can see the intent behind the voice and realise the integrity and sincerity behind the words is not malaise. It's just the self-worth line has been crossed and exposed and the lion has chosen to take responsibility for what he can do and speak up about what doesn't feel right only to be ridiculed and made a disgrace of. Does a lion not have a right to speak? Or do we need to learn the ways of a snake to be heard?

Just because I chose to find love for myself, just because I chose to speak up, just because I chose to create and require healthy boundaries for myself, does not make me a lion.

But in the case of having to choose who I would rather be, I would choose the lion (the one that spoke up) over the snake any day of my life. I am open and honest; I speak with my heart, and I love with it, too. What you see is what you get and that's my gift to those that I love—pure, honest, direct, loving truth, without agenda. The lion may be the obvious choice to pin things on in previous lifetimes, but not here in this 21st century. Today, we have the advantage of walking among a much more awakened and conscious state of humanity, where we are aware of the snakes.

I would rather die on my feet than live on my knees.

To anyone that has been subjected to gaslighting in any form, please know that my heart goes out to you. It is my firm belief anyone that makes you question your reality, your heart, your state of consciousness and has the nerve to misconstrue it, twist it and use it against you, is downright dangerous. Anyone that loves you unconditionally would never use this tactic on you. It's hard enough trying to find self-belief and self-worth while working out the reality of day-to-day situations that life forces us to face. Someone truly unkind, unloving an unsupportive that would use such an emotionally violent weapon like gaslighting is not worth having in your life. If they can do this once, they will do it again until it becomes their adopted language. They are tricks to gain power. When you're in a loving relationship, there is no power needed, period.

Blame

Verb

1. To blame someone for something is to hold them responsible for something negative that happened. To blame them is to say or believe that they did it or that it happened because of them.

What more is there to say? Blame is for the unaccountable, the unconscious and the plain disgraceful. We do not blame in our house. We have taught the boys from a very early age never to blame anyone for anything. To put it into childlike terms, "don't dob" as it shows weak character, unaccountability and creates the beginning of entitlement. There is a massive difference between dobbing and speaking up. To blame is to lie—to find a villain for you to look like a hero is both cunning and manipulative. Kids learn this behaviour from a young age, and it matures as they get older if not acknowledged or addressed.

Do you think blame is used as a resource in the marines? In the army? In the air force? When you think of the most honest, reliable and accountable jobs, these are what come to mind. Medals of honour aren't rewarded to those that find someone to blame and take no responsibility—it's quite the opposite.

When we pass blame, create blame or use blame as a weapon to self-protect, we are actually saying "I don't want to take any form of responsibility" or "some part of me wants to hide". It's in the approach of doing so that I ask the question, what is in you that needs protecting? What is in you that you don't want to see or own up to? Why does someone else need to take the fall for you?

Scapegoat
Noun

1. A person who is blamed for the wrongdoings, mistakes or faults of others, especially for reasons of expediency.

Don't do what I spent many years doing—taking on the blame even when it's not yours to take or finding a way to always be accountable for someone else's lessons. It doesn't matter what story you're led to believe and how much more superior the person tells you they are; it's never your birthright to take on someone's else issues.

I chose to take on others' issues in hopes that it would magically make everything better, that I would be seen as the good, respectful girl. My strategy was to stay focused on anything that I could be grateful for and to always show compassion to those that are struggling. If I keep focusing on the good in my life and scrape together the parts where I received love and joy, those moments would add up to form enough of a realisation that I could afford to take a few emotional and verbal hits every now and then. If it was coming from someone in the hierarchy, then wasn't that my job?

Natalie, 2021- Hell No!

Enmeshment

1. There is a lack of emotional and physical boundaries, you don't think about what is best for you nor what you want. It's always about pleasing or taking care of others. You feel responsible for other people's happiness and wellbeing.

In all my years of hairdressing, I have lost track of how many people have expressed to me how hard it is to do what truly makes them happy and be the version of themselves that feels right to them; to start a life with their new partner or take a different direction with their own new little family than the one they were shown. The condemnation and ridicule that comes with living an individual, independent life that consists of self-love, self-worth and the preservation of your own wellbeing comes at a very heavy price, for some. That is the ones that have come from being in an emmeshed relationship.

There is no such thing as independence and free will when you have been a part of an emmeshed relationship—it's quite the opposite. You are led to believe that you and the other person or people are one. Your feelings are the same, your pain is the same, your love is the same, your thoughts are the same. You're expected to know, think, see, feel, smell and hear the same. But the thing is, you're not the same, at all. What I have found to be accurate, as someone that has been a part of an emmeshed relationship, is that one of you is the dictator and the other one is the acceptor. There is nothing balanced, right or even human about an emmeshed relationship—it's merely a form of passive dictatorship. You are never free; your life is not your own.

Dictatorship

Noun

1. Form of government in which one person or a small group possesses absolute power without effective constitutional limitations.

The dictator is allowed to have no limitations, but the acceptor is not allowed one. If they kindly ask for one or spend their time trying to form some kind of boundaries to protect themselves, then an uproar of disgrace ignites. You don't go against a dictator; you just do exactly what you're told.

This is what I've spent many years doing. I didn't speak up; I just kept showing love and compassion because that person wore a name, a title, that was seen as much greater than mine. I was in no way entitled to speak from a place of honesty, kindness and love; it was still seen as disrespectful, and I was to be condemned otherwise. I was not an individual; I was one girl that was emmeshed with another. I was one girl that another was living through, who attached themselves to me, whether it felt right to me or not.

When I was a little girl, I thought this was what I was designed for. I didn't see how pleasing someone all of the time and taking care of their needs above my own could be so bad, especially when they took physical care of me. I felt like it was the least I could do. The thing is, that the little girl eventually grew up. She learnt things for herself. She experienced friendships, first-time love, seen the world for the first time and it lights her up in every cell of her body. One day, that same girl starts a business, gets married and has a family of her very own; she eventually creates a life of her very own. However, the person that the young girl was emmeshed with at a young age does not want it to be this way—they have not yet fully let go. The young girl spends her life still trying to accommodate the needs and desires of her emmeshed affiliate, all while trying to form a life of her own.

This has been my ultimate life challenge—to be seen for who I am, for my intentions, while trying to experience a life of my own. Trying profusely to show love and to exist both in two human worlds has been the monumental challenge of my lifetime. It has led me down the darkest of paths and made me question my reality, my identity and my sanity. I've been called names I never ever pictured myself to be; the defensiveness I have met, the tantrums I have pacified, the manipulations I have believed. And when they had nothing else to scrape the barrel with, they finally create a false narrative to share with anyone that is left to control.

The problem is that that young girl eventually became accountable for herself. She eventually started to listen to the voice within—the one that was there all along but instead chose to listen to the voice or voices of matriarchs. She was led to believe that your voice only matters in name of rank.

Hurt people hurt people, and I wasn't hurt enough yet to get knocked down and stay down, so I kept rising up until one day, I could not rise anymore.

Verbal Abuse

1. When someone repeatedly uses words to demean, frighten or control someone. Verbal and emotional abuse takes its toll.

Emotional Abuse

1. Can involve any of the following: verbal abuse: yelling at you, insulting or swearing at you; rejection: constantly rejecting your thoughts, ideas or opinions; gaslighting.

Here's the thing, abuse of any kind, whether physical, mental or emotional, is wrong on all and every level, full stop!

The thing about emotional abuse is that you can't physically see the scars, wounds and hits that you take—the emotional stabbing and internal bleeding caused from this. They are hidden on the inside with a physical façade that looks like everything is ok but, unfortunately, on the inside, it's not. You are left with wounds, battered and bruised and can be left with permanent scars.

No amount of bruise cream, ice packs or makeup can conceal the hurt emotional abuse can cause. A way through it is acknowledging that it is in fact verbal and emotional abuse. Then, decide if you want to become a victim to your circumstance, or if you want to heal and grow from it. One way is easy and the other takes lots and lots of work. I found it to be a challenging path; most of the time, I felt like I was walking it alone, which I was, because pulling myself out of darkness and despair is an individual process. I refer to feeling isolated while I was trying to heal my internal wounds; I was dealing with shame and condemnation for not surrendering to what the former hierarchy wanted of me simply because, one day, I decided to stop accepting being the scapegoat.

We all say hurtful things out of anger and frustration and things we wish to apologise for. But it's when you continually get told the same abusive words in a manner that makes you tremble to your core and want to melt out of existence that makes it unacceptable. There is an emotional line that just can't be crossed; when unloving souls go past that line, there really is no coming back.

When you ask them to stop, and they are in such a reactive mode that they can't seem to control their temper until you find a way of blaming yourself, that is not okay. When every cell in your body feels like passing out, your heart is beating so fast that you think it could just give out, and you could fall face-first on the cold floor, that is not okay. When you feel like all your F3 responses (Fight, Flight and Freeze) are triggered and you still manage to find some morsel of self-worth to defend yourself with, and you find the courage to say that you are worth loving, that someone out there wouldn't treat me like this, only to be told "You think you're so good, who do you think you are?" it's not okay.

Defensiveness
Noun

1. The quality of being anxious to challenge or avoid criticism.

2. Behaviour intended to defend or protect.

3. Defensiveness is a coping strategy where we attack another person in order to shift focus away from our own faults and insecurities.

"Defensiveness is the death to effective communication."
– Terri Cole

Let's face it, anyone that is being defensive does not want to engage in effective communication, because that would require real, honest and open communication; there's nowhere to hide and defensive people want to hide. They invest more time building up a wall of defence so they can hide behind it. The truth doesn't need hiding; perhaps lies do.

Engaging in effective communication would mean letting down your egoic wall of defence and putting down your position of superiority and get to the bottom of it. However, a lot of people don't want to get to the bottom of anything because that would mean that sometimes they are wrong. They don't want to be seen and exposed or held accountable for all or any part of anything. Here is where the big snowball effect of unconscious behaviour begins. I've always found it funny how defensive people want to be involved in the most thriving, loving and highly functional relationships, but are not willing to give out anything they wish to receive.

Defensiveness sets us up for competition—you versus me, making us unrelatable and on different sides of the line. I don't want to be on different sides of the line. Why can't I be on your side, and we just talk? Why can't we find some way to communicate without blame and defence? Surely, we don't have to talk all rainbows and butterflies all the time. Can we talk about issues that need to be addressed? Can we talk about feelings?

When you are in a relationship with someone that is shielding themselves with a defensive coping mechanism, you really have no way in—no way to be heard and no way of starting any form of conversation. I've spent years trying to infiltrate the wall of defence. I have tried strategies like writing letters and leaving them at the side of the bed, so I wasn't physically there; I figured I could write down what I wanted to say and have them read it without the person physically seeing me, hoping they wouldn't feel so attacked by my presence.

I even made a nice morning tea in which I laid out all these letters about what I admired about the person so they could see I wasn't attacking them. As I openly started talking about my feelings, whenever the person I was talking to got triggered or I sensed a moment of irritation, they would look down at the many nice words I had written about them so they could calm down, regroup and see that my intention is just to be heard and find a way to work through our challenges because, ultimately, I wanted to have a functional relationship with them.

Another strategy I tried was to go into the conversation and just listen to what they had to say and let them feel heard 95% of the time. Perhaps, that way, I could contribute a small but powerful message at the end and it would be enough. They would walk away feeling like they were in control of the conversation, which would make them feel like they were in the driver's seat. When they feel in control, then they don't feel attacked. When they don't feel attacked then I can be heard and they will see that I'm not trying to attack, that I just want to find a way to grow from this conflict and move forward.

No matter what I tried, I was always hoping to be seen for my true intentions. I was hoping to be seen as the girl that

I was—that I am. I hoped that if they let down the wall of defence, they would be reminded of the girl that has only ever held love, compassion and understanding for them.

The thing about trying to break that defensive wall is that you spend so much of your time and energy trying to break it that you haven't even begun the effective communication part yet. That's where they want you; that's where they keep you. They don't want to look past their shield at what's on the other side—a real, honest, deep conversation. It might be where you want to go but it's not where they do.

For the life of me, I don't want to do this. I don't want to be a part of this; I just want to find a way out. A way out that doesn't involve me sacrificing my soul and all that I believe I can be. – Natalie

So, what do you do? Where do you go from here? For me, I continued to go back for more, because of a name. If it was a friendship or a lover, I would have walked away a long time ago. But conditioning, manipulation, guilt condemnation, obligation and being shunned was the mixture of ingredients that mulled together to form the cocktail that I kept drinking. Whenever I had a glimpse of that internal "this doesn't feel right," "that's not right," it would be quickly replaced with another spoon-fed cocktail of shit.

There were times when I felt like perhaps making a loud noise and becoming a different person would work. However, trying to operate from a place of integrity was not going to get me anywhere; it only ever bought me time. I would find myself back in the same situation repeatedly. So, in any form, to stop what was going on, I tried injecting a large amount of assertiveness and dominance; I tried to match the verbal abuse with anger and dictatorship of my very own. I took my anger, hurt and frustration and reflected it back onto the person throwing it at me. I had created a shield of defence as I thought what they were throwing at me was really hurting and caused me pain; so, if I pick it up and throw it back at them, then they would know how it felt. They would feel the repercussions. Unfortunately, this whole approach backfired at me. It was doomed to fail from the start as it was inauthentic to the person I was. It was not how I operated, and my conscience got the better of me.

My attempt at being seen as the strong dictator of my own life—able to stand tall, speak loudly and stick up for myself—completely backfired. They were then able to use this approach as an emotional weapon by now labelling me as aggressive. "Look at you, look how aggressive you are." Because this approach was witnessed by others, it was enough evidence to make the rest of the people living under the same roof believe it, too. I was now seen as an aggressive girl.

What did I do? I overcompensated and became even more emotionally reserved to myself and my own needs. However, to the dictator, I became even more emotionally available; I wanted to prove that I wasn't what they were calling me. I didn't need to prove it to my friends, my co-workers, my boyfriend; they could see the girl I was and where my heart was. I wanted to prove it to the people that wore a name— people that lived in hierarchy; people that told me that they loved me since I was a little girl.

As I grew older and, I became, I guess, a bit wiser or more conscious of the fact that I was being emotionally controlled. I was not a child anymore, nor a teen; I was a fully grown adult who longed to think for herself. I wanted to still be seen as a kind, considerate girl, but the urge to stop being treated this way had grown stronger, especially when I was being treated so kindly and lovingly by people that didn't have a significant title in my life.

As one of my final attempts to break the wall of defence, I chose to combine my pure intention of wanting to come through this together on the other side, gathering all the love and compassion I could find, and remembering what I managed to receive throughout the breaks of unconsciousness. I spoke from a truly loving and honest place but took with me a firm and constructive voice—one that I was proud of. This approach felt right; it felt true to me and my soul and, when I walked away, I knew I would feel proud of myself, which I did.

That proud feeling only lasted a few seconds, though; as soon as they could see that I was talking from a place of unconditional love and high self-worth, they labelled me as sarcastic, rude and disrespectful.

So, what did I do? How did I feel? Mad, sad, and disappointed in myself. I was mad because it wasn't true what they were saying. I wasn't rude, I wasn't disrespectful. I was honestly speaking from a kind, unreactive place. The second point of call was to succumb to weakness and defeat and believe in what they were telling me—that's when I felt the disappointment. My heart would break—it would literally ache, and I would go cold inside and even have a slight shiver run down my body.

No matter what I tried, it was never enough. No matter what I did, I was never enough. It's at this vulnerable moment that I felt worthless, that I chose to curl up into a ball and hold myself tight so that it creates a shield of protection. I call this ball "The Grey Ball of Pain". My stomach would be in much pain, so much it would hurt to stand upright. My voice would go husky as it hurt to breathe; I sounded like a man when I spoke as it hurt to speak. In this ball (this feeling), this greyness, this coldness, the feeling of lifelessness, I would curl up to my knees, wrap my arms around my legs, bury my head in my chest and hold myself close. I would do this to form some kind of emotional shield around my heart around where I hold all my emotions. I would begin to mentally say, "Everything is going to be okay; I love you." I would repeat this, over and over, not believing any word of it. I did it because it's all I knew what to do. Like you would wrap your arms around a child, hold them and tell them that you love them and that everything is going to be ok, so I envisaged doing the same for myself. Hindsight, wisdom, accountability and doing the work has made me see that these Grey Ball moments are the largest pathways to growth and reaching places of personal strength you didn't even know existed.

You can blame me for the things that aren't my fault and have nothing to do with me. My ego may wear them, but my soul will not. – Natalie Falicz

Eventually, at the age of 36, my body officially gave in. Strategies had bought me time, but I was still living a life where I was constantly having to find them in order to keep this enmeshed relationship alive. Again, I chose to keep it alive because of the name of the person I was emmeshed with. I chose to keep finding ways to keep it alive because I was being manipulated (gaslit) into believing a narrative of myself that wasn't true. I believed that if anyone had the right to treat me badly, it was those that had the hierarchical name. I continually gave my power (unconditional love) away to people that took advantage of it, to people that were greedy and entitled and wanted more and more of it. They were entitled to it because of who they were and who they saw themselves to be.

I now realise (amongst many other things) that in thriving, functional relationships, entitlement doesn't exist.

So, 36 years later, my breaking point came. It only came because my soul had said, "Enough is enough, Natalie, you will not take anymore." After returning home from a family trip of a lifetime to the amazing Disneyland, I was greeted with a phone call that would mark the end of the enmeshed relationship I spent years trapped in.

At the time, I did not know it was going to be the end; I was on a Disneyland high and hoped to share my joy with the other person on the other end of the line. Unfortunately, I could only manage to say hello before I was met with enraged, built-up reactivity. It was a loaded phone call; the words that had unfolded took me by complete surprise. I didn't know what I could have possibly done wrong on my family trip to Disneyland—the happiest place on Earth. I certainly felt happy, refreshed and proud that both my husband and I were in a stage in our life where we could provide our kids a trip to such a place.

To be on the receiving end of a loaded, reactive, emotional missile once you've come back from meeting your childhood heroes, seeing your children elated every day with ridiculous amounts of joy, and having the time of your life, I was completely blindsided, to say the least.

Nevertheless, once I could catch my thoughts, I managed to stay as grounded and solid in my emotions as I could, figuring that the reactivity on the other end of the phone was intended to shake me up. Unfortunately, it did more than that. The most vulgar words were spat out at me and the tone in which they were directed sent spirals of shudders through my body. I thought I had heard it all before and that I had built up some form of resilience to what was being projected right into my heart. Unfortunately, I hadn't.

I quickly made my way somewhere that I could sit and compose myself, and that place was at the bottom of the stairs. As I listened to the endless efforts of the person on the other end trying to condemn me for actions, I did not even commit. I listened to them portray me to be nothing more than worthless scum, trying to implement guilt and shame for reasons I could not work out, not even pausing to catch a breath. There was so much hate, so much anger, so much festering resentment, waiting to unleash on a soul that would choose to wear all of it.

But not this time; not this soul. I would say it took all my strength to put a stop to the verbal abuse there and then, but I feel like on some level, it wasn't all me. To describe it to you would be similar to an out-of-body experience. My human body would go back for more, but my soul, my internal body, took over completely and I could see it happening the whole time. The alarm bells were going off and all the red flags had been turned upside down and on their heads. The emergency evacuation button had been pressed. I was to evacuate and get the hell out before it was going to destroy what was left of me for good.

I managed to protect a lot of me, and a lot of what I had spent years working hard to find. Unfortunately, when the phone call was over, I was not able to find my voice. As I pulled my trembling body off the stairs, I turned to my five-year-old son and told him, "Mummy is alright, everything is ok, sweetheart," but the words didn't come. My voice was gone—the life was knocked out of it. To say I got hit with an instant case of laryngitis would possibly describe it to some degree. The adrenaline in my body was the fuel that transported me up and down the hallway. I was in utter shock and disbelief. My human body wasn't running the ship this time—my internal compass was. I breathed and I breathed until I could connect with the Natalie I knew was on the inside.

Once I calmed down, I sat outside against our tall palm tree and continued to connect to within; I breathed in white light and breathed out stress and fear. Instead of telling myself everything was going to be ok, I felt like everything was going to be ok. For the first time, I realised that this unforeseen experience was not a part of the internal me—the part of me that resembles and reflects who I am. This was something that happened for me to learn and grow from. As soon as I got my head around the detachment of the situation, I started to feel better. Although I couldn't physically talk, I felt like I was on top of the situation, and I was therefore able to not allow it to escalate to a place of darkness and a place I would find myself not being able to get myself out of.

This phone call was life-changing for me, as was the experience. You'd think that after 36 years of verbal abuse, being called what feels like every negative name under the sun, you would somehow be used to it, like nothing you hear can shock you anymore. Well, when you've spent 36 years loving the person that says them to you, I can tell you, it does. The love creates a protective shield within itself that allows you to take the hits. It's wrong, I know, but I loved them and parts of me still do.

How many scars did we justify just because we loved the person holding the knife? – Anonymous

Over the years, I have developed a huge understanding that people who treat others this way are hurt people themselves. They are unhappy and they feel unloved and unheard.

For years, I tried to make them feel heard; I tried to make them happy. I realised their hurt and took their hurt on and tried to heal it for them or show them ways to heal it themselves. No matter what, I loved them through all of it. I loved them without conditions, but I did try and create emotional boundaries to cope.

The moment I lost my voice, was the moment I gained one. I have learnt not to stick my hand in fire and be upset when I get burnt. I chose to continue in a relationship with fire; I tried to heal the fire when it wanted me to, but the fire never truly wants to be healed, it just says it does. I have learnt that I am not one with the fire as I am not fire; I wasn't born to be fire nor was I born to take on the lessons of the fire.

"My loyalty kept me in some situations that common sense could have taken me out of."

Anonymous

Until I wake up and become conscious of this, I will always be playing someone's victim, which I know I am not. It's up to me to find love and respect for myself, not to give it up so freely to a name. It's up to me to remove myself from what does no good to my spirit.

I am accountable for me.

Sorry
Adjective

1. Feeling sad or destressed through sympathy with someone else's misfortune.

2. Feeling regret or penitence.

Apology
Noun

1. A regretful acknowledgement of an offence or failure.

2. An administration of error or discourtesy accompanied by an expression of regret.

3. True apology keeps the focus on your actions and not the persons response.

4. Sincere apology contains the words "I'm sorry" and is followed by the thing that happened. The words are important as they signify someone taking responsibility for what happened.

Empathy
Noun

1. The ability to understand and share the feelings of another.

2. Empathy heals wounds while apology merely acknowledges them. The ability to actually reach out

and touch the pain of another is necessary to achieve a deeper level of healing in a relationship.

You know something that just doesn't sit well with me and reeks of inauthenticity? It's someone's ability to physically say the word "sorry" and have no empathy, meaning or intention behind it. Not to mention they use it as a tactic; "I said I was sorry" like they physically opened their mouth, looked in your direction and the words came out, so they're in the clear as they can officially say they apologised.

An apology without change is just manipulation!

Amen to that!

I suppose someone needs to send those insincere people a letter explaining what sincerity is all about.

Sincerity
Noun

1. The absence of pretence, deceit, or hypocrisy.

2. Sincerity is the quality of being honest, true and real. An example of sincerity is a person who really means everything that he or she promises.

There is no denying that when someone is apologising to us, we are hoping that it is full of sincerity. When I'm apologising to someone, I am sure it is coming from a place of full sincerity, otherwise I wouldn't say it at all. While spending time doing a little research on the topic of apologising, I discovered that, for some people, it can be really difficult. They even describe it as "not an easy pill to swallow". While I have a very little understanding of this analogy, personally, I can't relate to it. I don't find it hard at all. Sometimes, I may feel a little embarrassed and ashamed, but I always feel the rewards far outweigh the embarrassment or discomfort you can get when apologising. It's not hard to say "I'm sorry" because I genuinely feel sorry for any harm or upset I have caused or contributed to. I want the situation to be better than staying in an upset, awkward place of limbo that can quickly turn into anger and resentment.

When I have done something wrong, I feel it all over my body; I'm wearing a feeling I don't want to belong to anymore. Admittedly, the disconnection from my true self and the misalignment with my ego took me there, so it's up to me to acknowledge that feeling and ask myself if I want to keep wearing it or send it back.

When I say sorry, I mean it with all of my heart; I mean it with all of who I am. I want the person to feel the relief and the love I hold for them. For me, "sorry" is something you feel, not hear. Sorry is something you show, not necessarily say. Your actions speak louder than words, but for me, and I believe most of us here in the 21st century, your actions speak louder, and so does your intent.

Intention

Noun

1. A thing intended; an aim or a plan.

2. The healing process of a wound.

Like anything in life, we need to get crystal clear about our intentions from the start. If we lie, deny or hide our true intention, we are never ever going to be in the place we want to be in. The place we spend all our time convincing others we want but never actually action our true intention ourselves, so we never find our way there.

Pride will cost you everything and leave you with nothing.

At the end of the day, you're either sorry or you're not. You either want it all to be ok and have that feeling of love back in your life or you don't. Sorry is not a tag, you're it approach: "I made contact, so now it's their turn". Sorry is not, "I just didn't know what to do, where to go from here". Sorry is not withholding love until you get treated in the way that your ego expects to be treated. That's just the point; there is no ego in sorry, there's just a feeling of unconditional love that pours through your heart and remembers how much you love the other person. It remembers why you loved them in the first place.

If you can't find it in you to apologise, then own it and be happy with your decision, because, ultimately, it is your decision.

Forgiveness
Noun

1. The action or process of forgiving or being forgiven.

2. Psychologists generally define forgiveness as a conscious, deliberate decision to release feelings of resentment or vengeance toward a person or group who has harmed you, regardless of whether they actually deserve your forgiveness.

3. Forgiveness is the choice that a person makes. Forgiveness is intentional and voluntary.

When I think of the word "forgiveness", I think of release, detachment and "no longer". No longer holding onto something that doesn't make you feel happy or holds you back. I have developed these feelings towards forgiveness over time; I did not see forgiveness like this when I was a young girl. For more than most of my life, forgiveness was the first thing I would want to access once I found myself in a disagreement, heated discussion or argument with not only a loved one, but anyone.

I didn't like the thought that I could make someone upset. I wanted that grey feeling to be over and I knew that I could make it all better if I said I was sorry, for my part. I always believed I did have a part in it, whether I did or didn't. If the person was unhappy, angry or sad and I was there, listening, speaking, doing, then I would somehow find myself feeling responsible for their emotions. I just wanted to make it better because the feeling of hurting or upsetting someone made me feel ashamed of myself. It made me feel like a bad person and I knew that wasn't my intention, so I did everything I knew to fix that awful feeling and the fastest way out of it was to say, "I'm sorry" and beg for forgiveness.

I would start by saying "I apologise if I have done something to make you feel that way," etc., and I would genuinely feel it and then spend the rest of the day or night accommodating the person's feelings.

If someone did something which required me to forgive them, I would be quick to instantly dismiss the apology and say, "no need, don't be silly, it's totally fine." Of course, I wanted it to be because I didn't like feeling like anyone owed me anything or I was in a more superior position of authority in which I required forgiveness. Growing up in certain environments, if I was to accept an apology, I would soon be punished for feeling so entitled to think that I deserved one. Sooner or later, their apology would be used against me with a "you think you're always right, who do you think you are?" I knew that was not a genuine, unintentional apology in the first place. So, for me, forgiveness was a place I wanted to set up camp and feel cosy in as soon as possible; I was offering it out like water in a desert

Nowadays, I have learnt to take forgiveness much more seriously. Instead of seeing it as something that I have an oversupply of and I can give it out at the drop of a hat, I have learnt to see value in my forgiveness and, most importantly, value myself. I am not a sponge nor am I a punching bag. I wasn't born to take on other people's mistakes and accept them for continually making them. A mistake is something you learn from, you evolve from. If you continue to do it, it is not a mistake. I made many mistakes when it came to forgiveness because I didn't require anyone to see forgiveness the way I saw forgiveness.

"Not everybody thinks like you, Natalie; people show things in different ways," I was repeatedly told. To the people that have never hurt you, the people that love you, forgiveness feels the same. For me, forgiveness is an intention. You can feel genuine intent. Forgiveness isn't complicated; it's simple. You either want to go there or you don't. If you do, your heart and intent will take you there. Your ego may stop you, but that's where consciousness can appear.

It doesn't matter what generation they were part of or how they grew up, if they are breathing this human air, walking this human life, having human discussions and existing as a part of humanity, they have the capability to switch the on button, wake up, learn and grow. It all starts with intention and intention is free.

No one is that special that they are not privy to intentions. The poorest, sickest, most mentally unstable person can still have intent. My beautiful Nonno (grandfather) was the sweetest, most beautiful man. His soul sparked joy in everyone everywhere, all the time. In his later life, he was unfortunately diagnosed with Parkinson's disease. Nonno began with slight shakes, which eventually emerged into paralysis in his legs as he was unable to walk. Not long after that, he was unable to eat, having to be fed through his belly by liquids. He went from a normal, functional, happy man to a vegetable that had no physical function but all of his internal function—paralysed by his physical body but yet fully conscious with intent.

It was here in this state I could see the true meaning of intention, of feelings of love. When I would visit him, Nonno would be smiling ear to ear; his spirit was alive and his willingness to look me in the eye without speaking and let me know he loves me, and he wishes me well will forever speak volumes of the beautiful man he was. His intentions on how he felt when he was around the ones he loved were clear. You could feel how he felt and how he wanted to make you feel and how he wanted to be remembered, even if that was the last time you were going to sit by his bed. There was more said and more felt with just his eyes and the intent he held behind them than some people spend their whole life using their physical body to express.

Intentions are your truth and forgiveness is held in truth. It's held in how you truly feel. Forgiveness is not a band-aid;

for if it is intended to pacify a situation, the same situation will come flinging right back at you, opening up and exposing a much deeper wound.

Nonno was yet another example of a man, my grandfather, who visibly sat higher up in the hierarchy but was never ever a part of it. When I was around him, we were equally heard, valued and loved. He accepted every part of me that I had to offer, and it was always enough. Ti amo Nonno, grazie per la tua gentilezza.

Acceptance
Noun

1. The process or fact of being received as adequate, valid, or acceptable.

Forgiving someone and accepting someone are two different concepts entirely, and acceptance is not forgiveness; it merely plays a small role in it.

There is no person in this life that doesn't want to be accepted for who they are, but that's not the type of acceptance I'm talking about here. I'm talking about the kind where you accept people for who they are but not how they treat you—accepting them but not their hurtful actions or unfortunate behaviour.

"Accept me as I am, faults and all, that way I don't have to change and take any form of responsibility; this is who I am and I'm not going to change, you need to accept me exactly as I am. My faults and mistreating are a part of who I am, so you either accept them or you don't accept me at all."

or

"I am happy to adapt parts of me that no longer work in this relationship. I do believe I have the ability to learn and grow and I happily make some compromise within my boundaries, things that need working on, in order to attain this relationship. I am not perfect; I have not reached a point in my life where I have mastered the best version of myself such that I no longer need to discover new ways of existing and evolving in an ever-changing world. There is no end to a human's ability to adapt evolve and grow. There are parts of me I don't accept, yet I require you to accept them so I can overlook them and live in an illusion as if they're not even there."

Here's the thing, most of the time, people accept the person but don't want to accept the mistreatment. The behaviour can be changed, nobody is asking the identity of the person to change. This is where I find that defence joins the party; by then, we have entered a whole different room—a room that has a staircase that spirals downwards. The mistreatment and the identity are two different components.

Judgement or criticism?

Judgement
Noun

1. The ability to make considered decisions or come to sensible conclusions.

Discernment
Noun

1. The ability to obtain sharp perception or to judge well.

I like to believe I exercise discernment on a daily basis. I see it as forming value and personal boundaries around my physical and mental wellbeing. I would be a lost soul without it as it is a human right to use discernment as a part of your life's toolkit. I certainly hope that my boys use it to develop a strong sense of self and to create for themselves a wonderful life that they enjoy being a part of.

To be honest, I'm ok with judgement or, should I say, being judged. Judgment is just an opinion, and although opinions can definitely hurt, people have a right to them. It's when those opinions or judgements are projected onto another that I see the problem in it. Don't project your judgement unless, perhaps, it was requested and valued. I find those that truly see me, know me and hold love for me don't judge me. I simply don't feel judged by the people I love and that love me.

I definitely have felt judged by the way I look, the colour of my hair, my size, the mother that I am, the person I am, and the list can go on. But at the bottom of all that, I just have to remind myself that those people don't know the real me. Even if they have been named a friend and can't seem to look past the nasty, critical judgements, then they are the ones missing out on everything I have to offer.

I am not for everyone, and if people can't look beyond superficial and external appearances, then their judgment is a blessing in disguise; you can choose to move on from that unpleasant feeling. That is why that form of judgment is critical.

What I don't like about the word is the misuse of it. When you communicate a personal boundary, for example,

"Could I ask you kindly not to smoke around my baby?" and they reply with a defensive snarl followed by, "You really shouldn't be judging me; babies have been brought up with smoke around them for years." Or when you spent the best part of an hour explaining how you are just simply two different people that think completely differently about the world and there is nothing wrong with that, and you don't succumb to their opinions, you get called judgemental.

Just because I don't agree with you doesn't make me judgemental. Just because I have a different way of doing things than you doesn't make me judgemental. My conclusions are simply my conclusions, they come from my heart all the way to my voice; once there, I make a choice to add volume or to silence the information.

There are people that know you are different and that you have a different way of doing things and they don't ask out of being genuinely interested, they ask to poke the bear and persuade you to convert to their way of seeing things. This agenda behind the question only results in judgement.

Again, opinions are a birthright, and so is discernment. We would be lying if we said we aren't all using it.

The Pain Body - Eckhart Tolle

If there was one book that could be put in every high school, university, college or human working environment around the globe, I would choose to put A New Earth by Eckhart Tolle. This book has had the most profound effect on my life. I feel like it is my human survival guide and the voice of the internal soul that tries so hard to reach us. While reading A New Earth, I was overwhelmed with relief. I felt like, for the first time in my life, someone was explaining feelings that I hadn't managed to find the words to express. I thought I would sound crazy and that no one would believe me if I spoke about life in this way. At first, it may seem complicated, but that couldn't be further from the truth. For me, it reads so clear and makes so much sense. If you allow yourself to read the words, with no ego involved, you will be pleasantly surprised to discover how naturally your body, mind and soul will soak up every word.

There were so many aspects of this book that had a significant effect on my life. By far, the largest was the Identification of The Pain Body. I will not get into full details as it is a broad topic in itself and one that Eckhart explains best with his own words. However, I would highly recommend you read and identify with it in your own personal way. In a nutshell, The Pain Body is the accumulation of old, unprocessed pain. The Pain Body is addicted to unhappiness, and it seeks emotional negativity. We all have one; it's only a matter of recognising it in oneself.

A New Earth taught me all about existing as a conscious and unconscious human being. When I am in my Pain

Body, I have switched over to unconsciousness. When I am in the state of unconsciousness, nothing good happens. Unconsciousness awakens the ego and places it in the driver's seat and, as I have learnt, the ego is "the false self". It reacts; it lives in suffering, and it needs more suffering to survive. Consciousness and awareness kill the ego; it brings you back into the present moment—the actuality of what really is. The Pain Body cannot tolerate the light of presence.

We are all light and we all have the state of consciousness in us—some are just operating at different levels of awareness. I choose to learn and grow from those that have the skills to master higher states of awareness as I believe the ego in me is a part of the human body, and a part of the human existence. Learning how to live with it or master it while living in human form, I believe, is part of mastering the human experience.

Will I ever master it? I don't know, but it is certainly my priority each and every day to put the effort in and try my best. From the moment I read Eckhart's book, it awakened something in me that I can't switch off—internal soul consciousness. I feel like I have a better awareness of when my consciousness is slipping and when the lights are dimming on my consciousness. Becoming aware that I have a Pain Body made me feel more responsible for the situations and circumstances I saw myself in. It made me realign with my true state of awareness and realise that when I was being emotionally triggered, I could watch the process happening, like an out-of-body experience or watching a dramatic movie play out. When I began to see life from this perspective, I felt detached from the negative, unconscious narrative that my ego was feeding me. The feeling of detachment made me feel safe and brought me back to the real me—the Natalie without the ego driving the mind's subconscious.

This all took work, and still does to this day, as I am human and still experience human unconsciousness in this life. I slip up, of course, but I must say that I learn from each slip up and developing this awareness has really helped build a protective, emotional shield to withstand unconscious behaviour both in others and in myself.

So, what do I do?

The thing is, we know what to do; the consciousness in us knows what to do, how to do it and when to do it. As cliché and generic as it may seem, you really do have all the answers within yourself to access at any time. It's a matter of believing in yourself and connecting to the present moment of what actually is, and not allowing your mind to drift off into the future where fear and uncertainty live. For me, it's a matter of realising how unconscious I allowed myself to go. If I have fallen so far from myself; I firstly identify with my false self and make a choice whether or not I want to remain like that or detach from it and be and want more than the unhappiness I'm choosing to sit in and identify myself with. This step is free, and you can do it. It may hurt, sting or burn your internal heart, but that's the ego and the unconscious mind trying to hold on tightly for dear life to all the negativity and unpleasantness it has created. Identify with it and you will break it.

"If you are not taking responsibility for your consciousness, you are not taking responsibility for your life." – Ekhart Tolle, *A New Life*

What do you do when you're in a relationship with a person who is at a different level of consciousness than you? Perhaps, I could ask, what do you do when you're in a relationship with someone that exists predominantly in their Pain Body and chooses not to take any form of responsibility for it or to become aware of it? What if this person wears a significant name or title in the life you were born into? What do you do then?

These questions were all that forever played out in my mind. These questions are the reason for this chapter and the meaning behind a name.

At first, I overlooked everything that I have previously mentioned in this chapter. I chose to overlook it all and stay unconscious to my feelings because I did not feel like the name of "daughter" was ranked highly enough in the hierarchy to express myself in my true form. In order of rank, where I was placed only allowed me to have a small percentage of voice. I tried using it to my full advantage when I could but, ultimately, it was only enough to witness that I had one, not actually hear and feel what I was trying to say. When I overstepped the line of my rank and used too much voice, I would be quickly deemed as disrespectful and to have stepped out of line, which I chose to believe I was.

It wasn't until reading A New Earth that I found such significant meaning to what was accruing around me all these years.

I spent years finding ways to deal with people's Pain Bodies so that I could be seen as a good, respectful girl and accepted into the hierarchy. Who was I, if I wasn't the identity the created for me? They knew what was best for me when I was unable to make conscious decisions, but there comes a point in life where human children, human people, learn consciousness and form their own identity and that's not a disrespectful thing, it's a human right. Why do we need to be deemed disrespectful and ostracised because of this?

The thing is, I was having a relationship with their Pain Body, their previously conditioned Pain Body that was most likely demonstrated to them. In some cases, they are portrayed, learned behaviours that the previous hierarchy instilled in them as a way of survival. Nevertheless, at some point in life, the unconscious mind has to want to change. It has to want to become aware. More importantly, it absolutely has to ability to become aware and create a new way of life—a new way of living, a new way of survival.

Eckhart's words have taught me that there is no way consciousness can reside in unconsciousness. Peace, joy, love and happiness do not live in a state of darkness. It is therefore my conclusion that if someone is constantly in that state, then no matter what part they play in life, title they have or name they hold, it is best to do your best and stay in the light. Work hard on keeping yourself there. Darkness has the ability to transmit into light, but we must understand that some humans just prefer to stay in the darkness permanently and simply don't know how to exist in it in order to have a relationship with it. To make the continuous choice to keep trying because of the name you hold is yet another form of me slipping into unconsciousness; into darkness. I can't keep protecting the sickness because it's making me sick and keeping me stuck there. When I make the conscious decision to be aware that this feeling is not my true essence and it's not who I am, only then will I find the unconditional love for myself and realise that I am light, and that light guides me out and returns me home where I belong. I reached this level of consciousness at the age of 36. I believe there are children that reach this at a much earlier stage in their life and it fills my heart with unimaginable hope and happiness.

I don't believe anyone should have to accept the darkness. I certainly don't want to offer it to anyone I love nor anyone I come in contact with. I don't want to be remembered for my darkness or my level of unconscious behaviour and my inability to have just the willingness to pull myself out of it.

I feel it in me; I know it's there. I'm no superhuman, but I will not allow it to define me. I will not allow it to rule me, and I will not allow it to determine and dictate my relationships.

I don't want to give my darkness to the people I love; I don't want to speak and operate from darkness. I would like to be remembered by my actions, my voice, the light that I contribute to the world and the people I love—not the darkness I chose to identify with and bestow onto others.

No one's name entitles them to bestow darkness onto another. Darkness is a choice, and so is light.

The Choice of Self-Respect

"The most direct way to stop someone from hurting you is to remove their permission from your own mind. No one can hurt you unless you are willing to accept pain." – Allan Cohen

I was absolutely willing to accept their pain. I believed from a very young age that it was law; it was seen as an act of love, and it was a service I was encouraged to provide. As a young girl, I hated seeing someone suffering emotionally. It felt like a part of my heart was being shattered into tiny pieces. I absolutely did not want to feel happy or experience joy when I knew that someone else was internally suffering. It didn't make any sense at all to be happy and playful if someone else wasn't. Seeing them physically unhappy deflated my soul and gave me no energy to move around lightly and joyfully. How can I go and play in the playground and not think about the person over by the swings that was sad? Even if they weren't in my line of sight, from a young age, I could feel their energy. In a classroom full of kids, I knew the ones that were scared, frightened, bullied and unhappy. I wanted to fix all of them at the cost of my own wellbeing. I wanted to let them know that even if they didn't know me well, that a simple "hello" and smile and a sign that I showed interest in them would be enough. I hoped that they'd know someone saw them, acknowledged them and that they did have a positive impact on me, which would ignite some form of self-worth in them, enabling them to see past the hurt they were sitting in.

Even when it came time later on in life, in my early teens, when I experienced passive bullying from girls, my first thought was to make excuses for their behaviour. "Everyone acts out of character; she is obviously having a bad day." I could see past the hurtful actions and see that there was more to them than the way they chose to behave. I knew that once they realised I was a person that looked beyond the physical aspect and saw the good in them, then they wouldn't feel the need to be that hurtful person.

As a young girl, I chose to focus on the good in everyone because that's what felt true and authentic to me. I was young and fresh, and I had emotional support to give, and I wanted to give it. It felt right, in my heart, to do so. Ultimately, I didn't want anyone to feel the way I did on the inside. Seeing someone not suffering gave me hope. It gave me visual proof that emotional freedom and true happiness does exists.

This may be an acceptable way of living as young child, but I believe if you are a human having a human experience, that experience will teach you that it is best to go wandering the forest with self-protection rather than live in the hope of your heart being the shield that will provide you full protection. In other words, it was a naïve way of living.

Life, in all its magical ways, has taught me to hold on to my heart, but also discover that it can be wrapped in self-respect and still able to shine in the same way I always wanted it to. It was in these moments with friends, high school boyfriends, work colleagues and in general, that I allowed the self-respect to protect my heart and still managed to create a balance of character that I would be remembered by. It was easier for me to value myself in situations like this because I didn't give all my power to them—that is, my heart. I believed there was only one place where my full heart was to go and that was where I was born into—to those that wore a name, a title. "I wouldn't be here if it wasn't for them; they gave me the biggest gift of life, so I owe them everything and all of me. My heart belongs to them; I just wear it." Red flag alert.

To be birthed into an environment that accepts a heart wrapped in self-respect and not be seen as disrespectful, dishonourable and condemned would be something I could only ever imagine. I am ok with imagining it as I have come to terms with where and what aspect of my life and my lessons are in. Ultimately, the lessons that may seem dark are more often the biggest gifts you can ever receive; so, there is polarity in imagining.

I will never regret finding respect for myself along my life's journey; I only regret lowering it or throwing it away completely to accommodate the people that saw it as a threat—to the people that wanted access straight to my heart. They believed that because of who they were, they had the right to it and, most importantly, I believed they had a right to it. I believed they owned it because they created it. Who was I to question the people that gave me life? Unlike like the kids in the school yard, I felt a hundred times more fiercely in love with them. I didn't want to see them hurt or suffering; it was way to excruciating for me to bear. I was more than happy to take on their hurt and pains; I just wanted the emotional suffering to stop and if that meant they needed access to all of my heart at any expense, conditioned or not, I would give it to them without question.

The truth is that this is extremely unhealthy; no one should want all of you and more. Nobody should need all of you like that. It should come as no surprise that living this way as a young girl was innocent and tolerable but growing up like this became a way to survive; a way to earn love and feel loved. It was completely dysfunctional, which is what I could feel but I couldn't explain. When I did, well, you know how that would go.

As I grew up, giving my whole heart became an expectation, a condition, that soon shaped the person I was seen as. It became my identity, partly created by my true intentions and mostly driven by the people that were entitled by name. The overuse of my heart became too much for me to bear; seeing the suffering and sadness go away used to be able to inject enough joy that it would suffice, but that joy began to dwindle when I began to feel used and taken for granted. I wasn't allowed to replenish and regenerate at times when my heart was relied on for their emotional survival. I needed to welcome some form of self-respect into my life, my heart, but every attempt at doing so only ended in the demise of my spirit and self-belief. I didn't want to hear how disrespectful I was and the hurtful words that came with the disgust that followed. It was much easier to pacify them with the only thing I knew worked, and that was more of me, more of my heart. The raw, exposed deepest parts of my soul's worth.

I felt emotionally stripped, so much that I became lost, unhappy and disconnected from my true self. I gave all of myself up until there was nothing left of me to give, and even at that point, I was still expected to extract whatever emotional support I could muster. I was an empty tank that began to malfunction. I was light that turned grey. I began experiencing panic attacks, health issues and entered into fearful thoughts. And I wasn't even 20 years old yet. I wish I believed in myself enough to know that just because of a name, that isn't enough of a reason to give over all of yourself. I wish I knew it wasn't my role to expose my vulnerability and have it taken advantage of.

"You knew I didn't want to see others suffer seeing how much suffering tore me apart and you took advantage of that and used it to free yourself from the pain you didn't want to experience. I was too young to wear that and I'm now too old to carry it."

"God does not ask you to sacrifice your wellbeing for that of another. Be valiant against thoughts and feelings that tell you that you can buy good for another at the expense of your own."

Allan Cohen

The lessons I have learnt around self-respect are invaluable. Just the fact that I know that such a thing can exist with people that carry a significant name, gives me relief and hope. I have learnt that self-respect is a choice; it's not something you can source externally through the validation of others—it's something you access within yourself. You have to find it yourself, and when you do, believe in yourself enough to know that you deserve to use it. Please, don't do what I did and give it away because of a name, because of conditioning or because of anything or anyone outside of you said. I was stuck because I couldn't find a way; I wasn't able to protect my wellbeing and give my heart and soul at the same time.

Your wellbeing is a priority; most importantly, your heart, your true, unconditional, conscious, deep part of your heart is not up for grabs. It's not cheap; it's unbelievably priceless. The problem lies not in those who take advantage of it but in us for not protecting it and exposing it to those that would only ever see the unbelievable value in it. We have a responsibility to ourselves to find it and connect to our self-worth, self-respect and to find value in the worth, love and wisdom we possess. No more will I ever sell myself for pennies when I know I'm worth more. No longer will I give my power (love) over to people that are powerless (loveless). No longer will I hold darkness in the light because of a name.

I have a name. I am not known from it. I have a meaning and it's called Natalie.

Part 7
Your Voice

"What I want from you is your voice."

Ursula

O nly once I began to heal and detach myself from playing the main lead in "The Good Girl Genre", was I then able to see life, people, humanity and myself in a different light. Because this journey was not an easy feat. I became very cautious not to fall back into familiar territories that would enable me to remove it again.

From this hyperalert perspective, I became conscious of the many ways humans silence one another through fear and manipulation. It's absolutely vile watching someone inject fear and doubt into someone's mind so they can control the outcome. Here, in this chapter, I expose this hidden agenda in circumstances that, from the outside, might be portrayed as sincerity. In fact, it's not; it's silencing, and all genders and all races experience it.

The voice I use today is far from the voice I spent the first part of my life using. Moving forward, I made the decision to turn up the volume, speak from heart, passion and integrity and with the confidence of knowing that, for the first time in my life, I honour the woman that I am.

The Good Girl Turned Voice Warrior

As innocent babies, we were birthed into this Earth to experience the human life. We were gifted these wonderful Earth suits, each one unique to its very own soul that it hosts. Some babies come into this world crying, others come it to it quietly and composed. Neither is right nor wrong; it just simply is. Whether you were born blessed with the gift of a voice or you were born without it, it's clear to say that you can and will be heard, regardless of circumstance. It is your birthright to be able to express yourself, however that may be.

I have learnt that your voice is one of the most vital and prolific assets of your human body. It can be used for bad, and it can be used for good. It is by far a magnificently powerful tool, and I believe every voice, spoken or unspoken, is powerful. Your voice speaks for your soul, it speaks for your mind, it speaks for your heart, and it speaks for your feelings and intentions; it's truly so incredible and can be used in the most incredible ways.

I have learnt that the value of someone's voice is priceless; no two voices are the same in any way. Voices are the most beautiful, unique and hand-crafted gifts that are placed inside the human body, ready to be released to the world. Although I am a firm believer that your intentions reflect your true voice and intentions can often speak louder than your voice, I also believe a voice speaking from the right intent and the place of integrity that backs up the actions makes for the most powerful voice of all.

I believe we all started off this way, speaking from pure intent, but through learned behaviours, being born into different environments and taking on different soul paths, we learn to express ourselves differently. We learned what felt comfortable to us, what felt right and what would be classed as acceptable.

In my early days of no-voice Natalie, I found joy in everything, and everything found joy in me. I spoke for nothing. Even if I wanted to go inside and play in my room instead of playing outside, I wouldn't say it because I didn't want to upset anyone, and I just wanted to make the lives of those around me easier for them. I took what I was given, and I was grateful for what I got. It was always enough for me, and I never felt like I was without. My voice was used purely for laughing, talking happily, providing comfort or not talking at all, and just enjoying life.

My childhood consisted of me being "The Good Girl" and the girl with no opinions, who doesn't matter, with no voice. Although I was extremely young, you could have seen my character. I believe character can be seen from as early as a toddler, or even a baby. Some characters are defiant, stubborn and already wanting to be heard, which I believe there is absolutely nothing wrong with that. I for one did not have those traits in my character, looking back I wonder if I had adopted some of them, they may have proven to serve me much better in the environment I found myself in.

As you can see, this was a dangerous and self-destructive way to live, even if I was too young to recognise it. I'm not now, and I don't put myself in situations where people want me to play the "The Good girl" part to accommodate their life's needs. A major part of my healing journey was realising that when you play small, keep quiet and the volume of your voice is either on low or mute, certain people become accustomed to you like that; some people even thrive off it. The world stays the same for us; nothing changes, and nothing gets heard and we stay in the comfort of "the safety zone". Here, nothing magical lives; only your fear and doubt. Placing yourself out of harm's way and out of upsetting or hurting anyone is just betraying your self-belief—a massive part of what makes you, you.

I want to make it clear that I am not talking about shouting loudly to be heard; it's not what I mean at all. As an example, I have a girlfriend that is soft-spoken; it would be out of character if she became loud and flamboyant. She is quiet and gentle, but her intent and voice are powerful and is heard when she speaks. You do not need to be loud to be heard; you need to be honest, authentic and put volume on what's true to you.

Realising that I had a voice and that I was allowed to express things that weren't all rainbows and unicorns was unfamiliar territory back then. But not now and not anymore. Finding the courage to speak up about situations that began to feel wrong to me was something that developed through years of healing and connecting to my self-worth. Back then, I found it challenging to find the strength to push through the guilt and shame of being titled as a disrespectful girl, shunned by my environment for speaking my true feelings. Now, I'm surrounded by people that value me for all of it— for speaking from my heart in everything and all that I do. They not only appreciate it, but they also love it as I equally value and love them deeply.

When you choose to live deep in the truth of who you are and put a voice to those feelings, it's like watching something truly magical happen; you attract people that love you for the truth of who you are and, better yet, they don't question it. They accept it and feel safe in it and want more off it. I could not be where I am at today it if I continued to keep my voice on mute, play the leading role in the people-pleasing, good girl genre and not realise my worth.

I have never been a disrespectful girl, just a girl with a voice and now, a woman with one.

Being Taken Advantage Of... So, That's a Thing?

Looking back and reflecting on where this all began when I was young and naïve, before I was even close to being a teenager, I remember my voice being frequently used to provide comfort, compassion and understanding. I was persuaded by love and by a name. In spite of my age, I had within me a maturity that much surpassed the age I was actually living. I was known and identified by this maturity and, as time went on, I was heavily relied on for it. At the time, I was happy to be seen this way as it felt right to me; it was my choice to give support to the ones I loved the most. Soon, this became my permanent identity and a requirement from me.

Many times, I would resist the urge to feel anything that was my own because all I knew was that what made me happy, what lit me up, what created my voice, detracted from their emotional needs and they came first. My voice was an expression of my opinions my conclusions and if they were different from the one I had been consistently providing them with, then there would be emotional punishment. This emotional punishment resulted in detachment, resentment and questioning of who I was if I was to be anything other than the voice they needed me to be, the words they needed to hear, the naïve voice of a young girl that had not yet reached adulthood. I provided a maturity that had become relied on by others much older than myself and I was needed for their emotional survival. What I needed to acknowledge back then, and what I will acknowledge now, is that I was being taken emotionally advantage of.

I allowed people to suck me dry and drink from my already bone-dry emotional tank—something I have never allowed to happen again. My reality was that, unless I found my voice and put volume to it, I was going to keep being taken advantage of. Today, my self-worth sends a very clear signal to my voice, which is on level 40 and shouts "not this time, not this girl!"

If anyone has ever felt like they have been taken advantage of, chances are your feelings are 100% correct. It's not a nice feeling and it's a completely obvious one. Many of us choose to do nothing about it because, a lot of the time, the people that are taking advantage of you are people close enough to know how to push your emotional buttons. Blackmail guilts you into giving up more of you. Why do we let them? Do they have the right?

The people that love me and want the best for me do not take advantage of my mind, body or soul. Simply put, they do not take from me, full stop. The reason they don't is because I don't allow them to anymore. The love I found for myself not only rejects anyone who tries, but also provides me with glasses to see through the façade (the ill intent) of what they are portraying. Just because somebody said they had pure intentions, doesn't necessarily mean they do.

I Shall Hide Behind Innocence, Then, I Can Poison You With My Apple

Sadly, there are many ways to silence someone and remove their voice. The most common way of silencing someone is often not the most obvious way at all. Intending to silence someone and take away their ability to access freedom of speech or allow them to speak only to manipulate and twist what they have said in order for your opinion to be heard, is an antagonistic trait. Like I mentioned in the previous chapter, this is done passively, like "a snake in the grass"—a trait that so many humans use to extract the good out of someone or something for their agenda to be seen, heard or put above the rest. By wanting to disempower someone through their mind, through their worth, and through their vulnerability, is a cowardly act and the sheer work of the devil. It's emotional abuse.

Below, I have listed a few examples of passive ways these villains remove, take and silence a voice. They are all done so cunningly and so manipulatively that the villain physically looks like they are in fact innocent and helping, when deep inside, they are working their dark magic to extract the one true thing they themselves are not—honest, pure and true.

I wanted to mention these characters because, so often, we find ourselves in situations like these when we question our own reality because we think these people are helping us and are in it with us. We think they have our best interest at heart, but, secretly, they don't; they just have themselves and their agendas as their number one priority. Because our brains don't operate like theirs, we think it unimaginable to even comprehend this type of behaviour, causing a lot of confusion in trying to rationalise that behaviour. What I've realised much later on in life was that I was completely naïve, and I had to wake up, grow up and learn that people do operate in this way that I never would imagine, and they do it under false pretences.

Ursula is a sea witch that claims to help poor merfolk through her own agenda. She is a manipulative, hurt woman that takes advantage of those that are innocent, naïve and choose to seek help in her dark magic. Ursula uses passive manipulation through a song "Poor Unfortunate Souls" to convince Ariel that she can help and give her what she wants. Although it may seem it's at a small cost using a form of gaslighting her way through music, she convinces Ariel that "it won't cost much, just your voice". This sounds innocent and convincing, which was the plan all along. So, Ariel decides to go ahead and make a choice. Ariel hands the most valuable possession over to Ursula by singing; she sings her beautiful soul-felt voice out of her body and into the hands of the manipulative sea witch. Once she is done, Ariel can no longer speak.

It doesn't matter how old I am, watching this part in the film, this process of Ariel's voice lifting up and floating out of her throat and into the hands of a dark soul, to own and control, leaves me feeling a heaviness in my own throat. Along with the feeling of hot tears welling up in my eyes, I feel heartbroken. There are honestly a few minutes where I feel a sense of emptiness inside, the feeling that I gave all of myself over because I was led to believe that it would all work out in my best interest.

Lady Tremaine plays the antagonist stepmom in the iconic film, Cinderella. Lady Tremaine was married to Cinderella's late father. Cinderella was left to live with her evil stepmother and her two stepsisters. Lady Tremaine resented Cinderella from the beginning for several reasons; one of them being the fact that the love her husband felt for his daughter never compared to the love he felt for her. Lady Tremaine kept Cinderella locked away, hidden in the castle, only allowing her to come up and enter the world as a servant to both her and her daughters' physical and emotional needs. Lady Tremaine knew her two daughters were naïve and selfish and had the makings of young antagonists, just like her, which is why they never posed a threat to her. Cinderella, however, was everything they were not; just by being her true self, the self she was born into this world to be, she was the mirror that shone a light to their darkness. Because of this, Cinderella was seen as a threat. Lady Tremaine abused her out of jealousy for her beauty and kindness. She hid these qualities away from the world and the prince, knowing full well he would welcome them with open arms. Cinderella would be living the life lady Tremaine ultimately wanted to live.

If seen Cinderella would be instantly valued, loved and treated the way in which she deserved, which posed a huge threat to Lady Tremaine. So, what better way to get rid of a threat than to hide it, speak down to it, keep Cinderella and her mind locked away? She manipulated Cinderella to the point of her believing that she had the best intentions at heart all while serving her own hidden agenda—a woman taking advantage of another woman's purity and innocence.

What happened when and if Cinderella spoke up? She was condemned and silenced, punished, locked away, unable to go to the ball. Not all of us have fairy godmothers (or item boxes) to rescue us; some of us have to walk the path of self-worth to discover that we deserve to be treated in much better ways. I must give credit to Cinderella as she never stopped believing in her dreams, no matter how she was treated. She never turned into a bitter, resentful woman and treated people the horrible way she was treated. Another example of a truly powerful woman.

Jealousy is such an evil curse in itself; I wish there was an antidote to counteract the vile poison it expels. I wish no such thing existed. I don't understand jealousy and I never want to, but it doesn't take away the baffled emotions I feel when I see an older woman, or a parent see light in youth as a threat.

The Evil Queen is Snow White's evil and vindictive stepmother who is obsessed with being "the fairest in the land". Because she is not, she becomes jealous of the young, beautiful princess. The Evil Queen concocts several plans to kill Snow White, one in which she hires a huntsman to do so. The huntsman takes pity on the young girl and cannot go through with it. When several plans fail, she resolves to disguising herself as an innocent old farmer's wife to manipulate Snow White into eating a poisoned apple, telling her that the apple is delicious, safe and will do her no harm.

According to literature scholars and psychologists, the story of Snow White is said to be a lesson for young children, warning against narcissism and pride.

The Evil Queen is an example of enraged, hidden agenda wanting to expel hurt, hence disempowering her, a threat; Snow White was the opposite of what she was—light. Some women see light as a threat which it never ever is. Light is unconditional love; nothing dark can live in light. Instead of trying to banish the light, she could have tried to realise the light existed within her, too. But this Evil Queen had fallen too far to regain consciousness as jealousy kept her in the dark.

Mother Gothel is a wicked crone who retained her youth for hundreds of years through the healing properties of a magical, golden flower. When the flower's powers are transformed through Rapunzel's hair, Gothel kidnaps the princess and locks her away in a secluded tower where her goal is to keep her hidden to take advantage of the healing powers within the princess' hair.

To do so, she cleverly poses as a kind yet overprotective mother figure that simply hopes to keep her daughter away from the outside world. Gothel is still extremely abusive despite her caring façade; she constantly insults Rapunzel, purposely lowers her self-esteem and riles up her anxiety with warnings of exaggerated dangers she could run into if she ever was to leave.

Of course, Gothel did this all for her own selfish gain. She is also known to victimize herself, blaming Rapunzel for any sort of conflict or unfortunate event that befalls their lives and relationship.

These women are all antagonists. Their equal resentment for anything outside of who or what they are was evident in the powerless way they chose to behave—to banish, lock up and hide away anything that posed a threat to themselves, to confuse someone's innocence and then take advantage of it. It's nothing short of evil; it's darkness and takes a dark, empty soul of suffer to implement such horrible strategies to try and gain the purity, the innocence and the lightness of an honest soul. To take advantage of someone's mind, of someone's heart, and twist it into believing in your way, another way, for your own personal gain, is inhumane.

These women did this and, thankfully, in the movies, did not succeed. However, in real life, for some of us, our ending never happened that way; we haven't yet broken free from the tower and are still living under the false façades and manipulative stories being fed to us. Perhaps, it's been too long to think or feel any other way. Perhaps, staying locked in a tower or hidden in a castle, only made to serve, is much safer than escaping to the unknown. What's outside the walls? The answer is: your worth.

"But these women keep us housed, clothed, fed and a roof over our head. Occasionally, they tell us they love us; I'd be crazy to leave and speak up about something that does not feel right." As each year begins to roll into another, you begin to lose your true self and become accustomed to the self that you needed to be to survive. Your thoughts are controlled, your emotions don't belong to you, you are what they need you to be, what they will accept you to be. You have completely lost the identity you were born with because someone else saw something in you that they need in order to enrich their lives. You belong to them, and you are at their disposal, born for their purpose, not yours.

I Escaped; My Fire Led The Way

I didn't escape until 36 years later. I found my way out of the tower, whether my human mind knew it or not. I had enough fire in me that could never be put out. When you've spent so long locked away in your mind, trapped by the constant pull of wanting to regain yourself and wanting to break free of the conditioned mind, when you manage to break physically free, you find yourself in the land of the unknown. Why would I want to enter into a land where I know nothing of? Because it's not yours (nor anyone's) path to suffer and live a life that was not meant for me.

My happily-ever-after comes each and every day I choose not to accept the way I was treated; to find a path to heal the generational trauma passed down and onto me. My happily-ever-after involves rediscovering who I am and spending each day reconnecting with the fire that still burns inside my heart.

There are days when guilt and shame try and seep their way into my consciousness, reminding me of how I "should" be and what would normally be required of me. These are little aftermaths of breaking free from old, conditioned ways of thinking. I have learnt to surrender to them and let life pass through them; if I hold onto what was, I won't move forward with what is. The deeper I learn to go with, the less I feel that way.

My objective is to keep the flame burning inside of me, adding kindling, stocking it with wood, keeping the flame of Natalie alive and well. I am responsible for that, and I am responsible for the conditions I subject the fire to. In order for me to keep the flame alive inside of me, I must stand for something. If I don't stand for anything, then I stand for nothing at all. While I was living in a tower, I stood for nothing; I had no opinions and no meanings. They were created for me, and I was naïve enough to believe them to be law.

The Silenced Male

You don't have to be female or a princess to understand the manipulative effect of having your identity tampered with and your voice silenced and taken completely away, leaving your mind and spirit so disempowered that you have so little worth that you don't even know who you are. As a form of coping, you just need to know who they need you to be to survive and stop more of the abuse.

Abuse is not gender selective. I don't care for facts and statistics; I care for the many male and female humans that have beared their hearts to me; the men I have known and seen subjected to emotional abuse. I care for the men I have loved, witnessed and watched suffer in silence. All forms of abuse are unacceptable, whether it's physical or emotional abuse, the brain takes the longest to recover. Yet, because some of us are fixated on what some—not all—men behave like, we forget that there are many men that feel and hurt the same way some of us women do.

I can tell you from experience I have seen men treated the same way as Cinderella, as Snow White, as Rapunzel. They have been locked away, imprisoned in their minds, captured, owned, manipulated and disempowered so much that they only access light when agreeing and enabling the women's agenda. I have stood by, watching their wings being clipped so they can only fly so far out of mental reach. I have seen men be emotionally castrated, dragged along by a disempowered chain of verbal and emotional abuse. Their lives are not their own; their lives are owned by a significant other. A toddler would have more self-worth and strength than the men I've seen subjected to this kind of abuse. Yet, on the same day, I saw him being told to man up, grow some balls, "be a man" from the same woman demanding chivalry, compassion and a soulmate.

I see men being disempowered daily in some sort of attempt to extract their voice, their ability to speak for the significant other to gain control. They seemed to be deprogrammed so some woman can program them into versions of themselves. We must remember that men are humans, too, and some of them, just like some of us (not all of us), hurt, feel and care like we do. It's not them versus us or us versus them. We are both powerful and have the ability to hurt, control, disempower. It's nice to be reminded that we may be different but we are all having a human experience and therefore we are all privy to all the good and bad emotions.

I was fortunate enough to keep my fire alive in me; unfortunately, for the men I have witnessed and the particular ones I have loved, it has broken my heart to see their fire burn out. Their souls have died; they now only live to exist in human form. They're living on the outside but have deceased on the inside.

The brain is a powerful muscle; who are we without it? The heart is a powerful muscle; who are we without it? When someone's target is to own our rights and we willingly hand them over out of fear, what or how much is left of us?

As men and women, it is our right to speak up about abuse and mistreatment, no matter who it is coming from. Speak up before you sink into that place where you believe you deserve to be spoken to that way. Speak up before there comes a time when you make excuses and find reasons to justify their behaviour. Any sound makes a massive wave, so make a sound and speak up out of love for yourself. A voice spoken through the channel of love travels further than a voice spoken through hate or agenda. When you find it in your heart to connect to the love you have had inside you since birth, you will find the confidence to speak your story, your truth—the truth of who you are can never be lost, only forgotten. What you forget is there to be remembered.

You are your way out, which can feel scary as hell, isolating and alone, but only for a short time. There is so much warmth and love waiting for you outside of your conditioned mind. Life is waiting for you on the other side.

To the silenced male,

Don't look at past hurts; don't look at future expectations; don't look at what current gender issues are trending. Be the you that you are on the inside, away from all the noise. There are a lot of women that see your heart and would never take advantage of you. There is a need for you and that's why you were birthed into this life. Just because you wear a different suit than me (a different gender), doesn't mean you are the enemy, and I am the victim. Many that have worn your suit have been the enemy, but many have also not. Remember, enemies come in both genders. I will not judge what others have done; I will only go by what actions you have shown me and the intention I feel radiate from your heart. I am a powerful woman; therefore, I know I live amongst powerful men, and that's nothing to fear.

Your heart will always be welcomed by other powerful beings.

Love, Natalie

Intention Vs Agenda: What Team Are You Really On?

We all have intentions, good and bad. They exist within us. Intent is what drives us to take action on things, to speak up and to show up as who we are. We intend to get ourselves out of bed in the morning; we intend to do well in our team sport or to deliver an inspiring speech. We intend to wish our loved ones a happy birthday, and we intend to do well in a course. Intention drives us and steers us into a direction that we choose to exist in. However, a visual display of a good action doesn't mean it has good intent hidden beneath it.

Growing up, I may not have been brave enough to voice my concerns, opinions and views, but I sure as hell could feel them. They were held within the feeling that what I was seeing didn't always represent what they portrayed. I also have never liked anything being projected onto me as if I was the devil if I didn't believe it or swallow what was being spoon feed to me.

As contrary as it may sound, I have learnt that part of discovering my voice is learning how and when to use it. I have been able to see that speaking with true, honest intent that exposes a truth without a hidden agenda is the most powerful and profound way to speak. Intention that has the foundation to inform people with unbiased facts in order to shed light on a specific topic, to open up discussion that may lead to a way of improving, helping or enhancing a cause or circumstance, seems to be the most integral and effective way to be heard and make a difference. At least, this is what I have to remind myself of. I have been guilty of my ego and agenda wanting to take a hold of any common sense, causing me to find myself having to realign with my true intentions which is always to be of help or help the situation. That just can't be done if I have a hidden agenda and projection hidden behind my help.

Reactivity kills good intent. As you know, I am all for extracting the voice. However, birthing it into a reactive environment and operating from that space is never a good idea. Mr and Mrs Ego run that town; my perspective would be ruled by the fact that I just want to be heard, seen and my point valued. We all want that, but there are better ways of going about it than it being fear and ego driven. A forced agenda pushed down anyone's throat is self-serving, selfish and detracts from the valid point we are trying to communicate. Opinions are someone's thoughts; opinion is not law—no matter how many people stand behind the opinion, numbers don't make it official. Unlike the 21st century that I am currently living in, the amount of likes and the amount of hits, feeds, etc. make us believe otherwise. We need to remember that life exists outside of those likes and it is far greater than the feed you're consciously and subconsciously looking at.

I believe a vast majority of us, when we are watching someone preaching to us about a topic, be it political, environmental, social, etc., we can feel if that person is speaking with real passion, heart and conviction, or if it's just a robotic, mainstream, generic on-trend speech that has a hidden agenda behind it. People are able to feel integrity; they feel passion and someone's desire to express honest emotion, but forget the voice driven by agenda and self-serving intent. That voice doesn't last long; it comes as fast as it goes, leaving no impact and serving no one but the person throwing it out there. We always have to remind ourselves why we do what we do, who we do it for and what our true intentions are because we are human. That human nature likes to pull us in the opposite direction of consciousness and off our true, internal light. Our innate soul doesn't lie, but our Earth suit can get caught up in the human experience and in the human mind. That same mind that can get caught up in resources that are put here to help, like social media, news, etc., to which, if we are overexposed, we run the risk of either imploding or becoming side-tracked from our true purpose. In many cases, we can become brainwashed into hysteria and, worse, end up following what portrays itself to be "the majority".

On-Trend or Timeless

Today, I watched one of my mentors, inspiring mother, author and speaker, an amazing woman that has worked her butt off to get where she is be absolutely ridiculed for openly and honestly communicating how happy she is to reach that point in life. I watched her openly communicate her success by stating how hard she worked to get there and what a great honour it is to be living her life in such a magnificent way. I was extremely inspired; her intention was honest, pure and came from a place of sincerity. She was expressing herself in a humble and informative way and in a manner that many of us can aspire to.

Unfortunately, she was met with an extreme amount of unpleasantness as she was ridiculed for her delivery, her success and the specific word choice that triggered the current on trend, "victim mentality". She was overseen for her intent that all her loved ones, friends and genuine conscious followers know and love her for. Instead, she was discriminated for all of it because, currently, speaking up and voicing anything that is not of suffering or sacrifice is not on-trend. She was seen as "privileged", which is a label and a name in itself and is often used to discriminate. At times, it seems that if you are not suffering, then you are privileged, and if you are the creator of privileged circumstances, then you are discriminated and shunned and socially crucified and blamed for not being compassionate. You are a monster to other humans who aren't suffering. Whether you're creating privilege in your life, or you already come from some form of privilege, it's not pleasant being discriminated against for it.

Privilege shouldn't be used as a weapon to demoralise people and their circumstances—to bring them down from where they came from so it's an even playing field. The reality is that it's not; we don't have equal playing fields. Life, here on Earth, wasn't designed for that. We don't all start at the same starting line. As I mentioned before, we all have different item boxes and access to them; some, none at all. Some of us get handed the life raft and others have to build from scratch. Some may have to even look for parts before they can even begin to build.

There has been a major area in my life where my husband and I have had to find our own parts and build a life raft, with no instruction manual. I have never looked over to those that were handed a luxuriously built life raft and seen their "privileged circumstance" as a way to highlight what I don't have and what I went without. In fact, I have learnt to see the setback and my longer road ahead as a priceless tool that will guide me through the rest of my life. In other words, our setback, the harder road, the unfortunate circumstances that our soul has signed up for are our greatest allies, teachers and tools that make us unique. We all have things we can be grateful for It comes down to prospective. We must not forget someone that may physically appear to be in a less privileged place may be freer in mind and heart than someone that presents to be privileged I guess it perhaps comes down to what we individually define privilege to be.

Hate won't fix hate; treating someone how you were treated will solve nothing. Punishing someone because you were punished creates a powerless mentality. Speaking up from resentment only creates a deeper wound. Hurt people, hurt people and then create a victim mentality, which enables a victim following. This type of following attracts all the other fear-based, unhappy humans. Suffering follows suffering. That following generates millions of likes, millions of followers and attracts what feels like "the majority". It's not—it's just hysteria and social media that is so easily accessible. The thing is, it's not social media to blame here, it's our discipline with it—the social media platforms. It's no different to sugar or alcohol; it's up to us to balance the influence it has on us. We are accountable for how much we submit ourselves to it and start believing what we continually subject our eyes and our minds to.

We must not forget that, if there is a subject that we are passionate about, there are many historical books, many different records and other practical resources for information other than what's trending on a feed. History will give us a much clearer, slower, longer, more in-depth, detailed perspective on life; social media will give you a fast, biased agenda imposed on trend perspective.

I am very sensitive to social media—I can take a lot less of it than the average human. I do see it as a way forward as there are many wonderful things about it, especially for business purposes. Everyone gets their source of information from many different places, but I choose to get mine from podcasts, books, in-person consultations, events and people who have lived in the history of the times. On one hand, there is history, and on the other, there is hysteria. I, for one, cannot stand hysteria and victim mentality and fear-based headlines and, worse, people capitalising on that hysteria and breeding more of it into the world. We are desensitising the nation to the point of silencing humans with fear so that they stay silent and obey. Where I live, they are currently removing iconic childhood names from candy wrappers, foods and renaming TV shows that I enjoyed growing up, wiping out years of memories. Instead of facing the problems and opening up pathways for future decisions, we are removing it completely.

I honestly feel like if you're not suffering, you're not conforming. If you're not playing the victim, you're an insensitive human. There seems to be no rational, common ground. I believe in shining a light, not burning a hole. Speaking and informing people and educating people from an act of love and service are going to make real change in the world, like Nelson Mandela, Mother Teresa, Princess Diana, whose timeless voices and messages spoken with the voice of good intent of service and no agenda.

We must not shun people that have worked their asses off to get where they are, no matter what race, gender, belief system or size. Even those that were born into an endless supply of life rafts and item boxes shouldn't be discouraged for it. We have to stop putting down what we think is above us, including Victoria Secret models, people that fly in first class, mothers that have babies that sleep through the night, people that have supportive grandparents that are available to help with kids, etc. I would argue with anyone that just got off a long flight in first class and said that that wouldn't be the preferred way to fly. Money, success, social media, people that don't have to diet and luxuries aren't the problem; the way we view them and the opinions based on or own insecurities are. There are a lot of genuine people that are not identified by their circumstances. The problem is on the inside and it's on the inside of us. We must not silence success, beauty or people that didn't have to struggle to achieve something; we must not silence, full stop!

People enjoy a good underdog story—someone rising from the very bottom to the top—but I also like hearing about people that have simply succeeded, even if they came from privileged backgrounds and began from the top. I would never discriminate who is entitled to success and who is not. Success, greatness and the right to happiness have the right to fall into anyone hands, privileged or not. We all have to work hard for things, in all areas. There are a million different aspects to life, and no one gets all boxes ticked in every single one of them. We all have our own battles and lessons—no one gets a get-out-of-jail-free card on that. It's the battles we face and how we choose to face them which defines our experience. We can either learn and grow, or we can become victims of our circumstances and live in suffering.

Our voices can be our greatest tool to lift us into the light. Communication is key, which is why so many try and take it away from us. Don't let them; speak with love and speak with the pure intent to help and honour your soul's voice. Our souls are always operating from a higher place of good; we just only need to remember how to reconnect with it. Your voice has the gift to be timeless and leave a legacy and in order to achieve that, it has to be from love.

Don't Be Afraid: Haters Gonna Hate, And That's a Good Thing

I'd like to start by saying that "hate" is a strong word; it's a word I don't like to use but, here, in this context, I have chosen it to represent a large group of people you may or may not have encountered in your life. For example, haters, to me, comprise anyone that wishes ill towards you. Haters are people that don't have your best interest at heart and that misconstrues anything and everything you say in a way that brings you down and places themselves and their point above yours. Also, "haters" is another name for bullies, liars and generally just unpleasant people. They are even known as "trolls" nowadays.

Here's the thing, haters are doing their job, they're hating for whatever reason they choose, to live a life so colourless and grey, and the best thing we can do is let them. Don't take any part in it because, ultimately, you're not a part of it. It's something going on inside of them and it's separate from you. Through time, I have learnt to appreciate them; they are a constant reminder of not only where I never want to be, but of how far I have come. If it wasn't for them, I wouldn't have learnt what pain feels like, what suffering feels like and what it's like to wake up out of insecurity and into my warrior voice.

They will always be there, but the deeper I go within myself, the deeper I root myself into the ground, into the core of Mother Earth, the less effect they have on me. Haters are people that haven't yet acknowledged the light and love that exist inside of them. They haven't begun healing; so, instead of doing something long, hard and warrior-like, they choose the easy, quick path of hate. If it wasn't for people like this reminding us of who we really are, (love and light) we might forget.

I now know what it's like to live a life full of wonderful, uplifting, soul-supportive, undyingly loving people that love me for me and the voice that speaks through me. But it's not until I am reintroduced into the unpleasantness of hate that I really get the awesome reminder of how far I have come and how far from that unpleasantness I am. They are a mirror of grey, and for the first time in my life, I get to look at that mirror and see nothing but light—the light of who I am. So, it is here where I say thank you to all the haters in the past and the ones that may come in the future. You are the reminders of my worth. You are the reminders of the value I found within me. You are the reminder that I found my voice; and where I take that voice is endless. Your hate only fuels the ever-growing love I have found for myself, and I will never spend another day living without it.

To you, the reader of this book, I promise you with all that I am that there is a mountain of love and light that radiates inside of who you are. There are many people that want to love, nurture and support that love. Please, don't ever let any person silence your voice of love, truth and pure intent. The world sees truth; they hear truth. Truth sticks and truth impacts. Your soul truth is what attracts the greatest love—the love you have been yearning for. A voice spoken from love and from heart is a voice worth fighting for; it's those that have found that love within themselves that will help guide you on your path. These people become your soul family, your soul friends, your soul loves. These people are my Soul Army, and they provide me endless love and support, these very special people are mentioned at the end of this book. Today, I stand tall knowing I only engage in what I call "frontline relationships"—people that I would fight for and people that I would die for. I know these people would do the same for me. It's a liberating feeling to exist in this way, and to be honest I owed it to my self-worth a long time ago.

So, speak up, regardless of your exterior; it's better to try than not try at all. You are a leader and leaders fall. But you know what makes us leaders? We get back up when we fall; we got off our butts and can say we tried rather than not trying at all. The universe always rewards courage, and I guarantee it's the gold that exists inside of you. Shine your gold into this life; it's needed now more than ever.

Conclusion: The Kingdom Worth Fighting For

"We all have things we are fighting for. We all have battles we need to fight, whether it be a battle within our minds, our environments, our relationships, or the lands we live. No one is privy to ultimate privilege. We all have battle scars, wounds and our own mountains to climb, some higher than others, some lower than others, but ultimately here in this human life, we all climb. We all own armour, we all suit up, ready for challenges, known and unknown, that lay ahead of us. How we choose to see those battles and how we choose to fight the battles define who we are and the legacy we leave. Discovering that you are the creator of the ultimate kingdom, the kingdom that is existence of the discovery of your own self-worth, your own soul's voice and your desire to live in all your integrity and all of who you are. This kingdom houses the greatest castle of all time, that castle is you."

-NF

You are timeless, I am timeless; we are all going to move onto the next life after this one. No matter where that is for you or what your religion is, we all have a place to go to after this human experience. The way I view it is that each of us is here in this life, experiencing different kingdoms. These kingdoms are placed all around the world. Inside these kingdoms are castles; they are all uniquely handcrafted and magnificently built. No two castles look the same. They are all stunning in their own unique beauty, and they are all built for a reason and carry inside them a purpose. They all carry self-love and endless amounts of self-worth.

I like thinking of myself as a castle. It wasn't until writing the end of this book and reflecting on all I have endured and reflecting on what I have written that I have come to this conclusion. What I have always known to be true is that, although we are all different, we all have very similar experiences that we can relate to on some level. Using a castle as a metaphor to define my current human experience thus far made me acknowledge that I, in fact, was the creator of my very own kingdom. Most importantly, I realised I was a kingdom, and one worth fighting for.

I see my body as the castle built inside a kingdom (a world, a life, I have chosen to accept and created by choice). I acknowledge that I allowed every and anyone to come right in and set up residency right in the inner ward (the centre of the castle, my heart space). I allowed people access right into my heart space—the most sacred place of all. A place I now only accept for the ones that are worthy and know how to honour it. I have learnt that name or no name, title or significance, that people who don't unconditionally value and honour both the castle and the kingdom need to take their place outside the walls. That way, if they throw stones, breathe fire or launch their cannons, I will be better protected having purposely built a fought around my castle (my heart), ensuring I will be forever sheltered from harm that wishes to come my way.

I am proud that I came to the conclusion that I am solely responsible for building and maintaining the structural integrity of my fort of protection. I am proud that I have come to the realisation that I am worth protecting and that I am worth fighting for, even if it's only me fighting for myself. I will keep my internal kingdom thriving and alive.

My goal is to be an example for my children; for them to realise that we have all the strength and courage inside of us to fight for our self-belief, to fight with courage and honour to maintain connected to our self-worth to our value. You are a kingdom worth fighting for. You have the final say of who enters your kingdom and who has the right to enter your castle, your heart space, your body, your mind and your soul. We are kings and queens of our life and our destiny. It's not up to anyone else to fight our battles; it's up to us to rise up and be victorious in our own, that way we can gain more courage for the next. We can be true examples of accountability and strength.

Life is full of lessons; it's one big journey, it's what you make of it, and it's what you take out of it.

Our lives are no one's responsibility but our own. I wish to leave a legacy and the only way to do that is to honour my truth and live by example. I know for certain that I work hard every day to leave a memory of a castle that was built with solid foundations which consisted of unconditional love, support, honesty, hard work, determination, accountability, trust, the ability to speak freely and use your voice, and by all means, to leave a legacy of emotional freedom, physical freedom—freedom of all and every form.

Freedom for my boys to live a life free of conditions; for Ashton and Travis to be able to wake up each day and know they are enough just because of the fact that they opened their eyes and drew breath. Freedom for them to rise to the freeing feeling that they can be who they want, love who they want, live where they want, and not have to live under expectations. Free to live in their own lane and not be pulled across and dragged under by anyone, especially those that hold a name. Truthfully, I wish that for all of you. I wish for your physical or emotional freedom. Whether it be from a person, a place or from your own mind, my wish is for you to find the peace that exists in your heart; to find ways back to you, to know that you have all the resources inside of you to build the most magnificent kingdom of all time—the kingdom of you. We are kingdoms worth fighting for. We are always more than we are led to believe. So, instead of being led, you lead the way.

Resources

Melissa Ambrosini – Mastering Your Mean Girl

Melissa Ambrosini – Open Wide

Melissa Ambrosini – Comparisonitis

The Melissa Ambrosini Show – Podcast

Melissa Ambrosini – Instagram

The Nick Broadhurst Show – Podcast

Nick Broadhurst – Instagram

Eckhart Tolle – A new Earth

Alan Cohen – Dare to be Yourself

Emily Gowor – Born Great, The Write State of Mind

Rebecca Campbell – Rise, Sister, Rise

Inna Segal – The Secret Language of Your Body

Evy Poumpouras – Becoming Built Proof

Judith Orloff – The Empath's Survival Guide

Paulo Coelho – The Alchemist

Rachael Hollis – Girl, Stop Apologising

Louise L Hay – You Can Heal Your Life

Louise L Hay – The Power is Within You

Kute Blackson – Podcast Soul Talk

Kim Anami – Podcast Orgasmic Enlightenment

Jim Kwik – Kwik Brain Podcast, Instagram

Wim Hoff – Instagram

Lisa Bilyeu – Instagram

Gregory Dunn-Smith – Bespoke Acupuncture and Healing

James Hand – Maps for the Journey

Dr Gerry Flynn & Alan Patching – Imprints for success

Dr Gerry Flynn – Sleep Fun

Peta Kelly – Earth is Hiring

Dr Shefali Tsabary – Instagram

Terri Cole – Instagram, podcast The Terri Cole Show

Revie Jane – Instagram podcast, empowered with revie

Acknowledgements

To all my life-changing and remarkable clients of the past 20 years, I have learnt more from you than I could ever repay you for. Thank you for teaching me. Thank you for holding space for me. Thank you for seeing me. Thank you for hearing me. Thank you for being authentically you. Thank you for the quality of your conversations; you have been some of the most amazing teachers of my life. I have listened to your words, "Natalie, share your voice with the world." So, here it is, my voice that I found and placed into the pages of this book.

To all my incredibly beautiful friends that encouraged me to pursue my dreams and believed that I would get here, I look up to you so much. Your successes and your journeys light me up and fill my soul with joy. I am extremely grateful for your friendship, your love and support, and for seeing my worth when I couldn't. You are part of my emotional support team and with that love, support and encouragement, I have been able to produce a book I am truly proud of.

Emily Gowor, it feels like a lifetime ago that we had our first encounter in the busy Brisbane city café. To think I would be here at this point, writing acknowledgements at the end of my first book and to be sitting here, writing as a different woman—you had mentioned that may happen. I want to thank you for being the beginning of this incredible life-altering journey. You provided me a door that you so graciously opened; and since opening that door, you allowed me to take one of my most powerful possessions with me—my voice. You stood back and allowed me space to open up my depth without interference or influence.

The sheer fact that you see the book-writing process as a mind, body and soul experience, allowed me to bring together all parts of me and to open up to the core of who I am and feel confident enough to write about it, which is exactly where I wanted this book to come from—my core. Emily, there was a flame inside of you that kept me warm throughout this process and that flame is your passion for wanting people to believe in who they are and that they have the capability to fulfill the purpose of who they are, however that may come across. It was with this passion I was encouraged to open up and write all parts of me. I was able to write everything I have ever wanted to say. Thank you, with all my heart. I will forever be grateful for your internal flame.

To beautiful Mama Rae (aka, my fairy godmother or, shall I say, everyone's fairy godmother), you are one of life's most beautiful treasures. Besides your unbelievable soul-healing cooking that nourished me from the inside out, you have the most beautiful and rearrest heart I had ever encountered. The very first time I met you, you wrapped your arm around me, looked me deep in my eyes and smiled at me with a love that was so pure, I felt even worthy of it.

You continued to look at me, embrace me, in this stare and through this love that you were so wonderfully generating into my heart. I felt loved, I felt seen, and I felt special. You looked at me like you believed in me and that I had the power to do this. Thank you for gifting me your love. You are one of the most powerful people I know, and, by the way, I totally believe you have magical powers and have secret magic dust because you are this world's fairy godmother. The power in your eyes, in your heart, in your love was the magic dust that helped me believe in my journey ahead. I love you, Rae.

To my magnificent healing team and all the incredible healers that have been a part of returning "Natalie" to wholeness. It took a team and, I am proud of myself for finding the right help. I couldn't do this on my own, and for that, I would like to say a massive heart- and soul-felt thank you to:

Greg Aus Acu Acupuncture and healing. Greg, you are one of this life's most powerful leaders. Earth is very blessed to have you in it, as am I. Healing with you is like a journey in time, space or another land, which is exactly what I needed in order to remember who I am and where I came from. I can't thank you enough for being exactly who you are and living in your power. I usually meet people that I feel I have had a previous past life with, but with you, I feel we are going to join forces in future ones, too, and I can't wait. Thank you for realigning me and offering your voice and wisdom along the way. Thank you for all your support. You are truly magnificent and very much loved.

James, my psychologist, you are a being of your own class. Anyone who is blessed enough to come into your genuine and loving presence is a person truly healed for life. You are one of the most beautiful human beings I have ever met (although, I believe you're more soul than human). I can't thank you enough for just being exactly you. I have reached many heights learning your teachings because you made me see what I already had existing inside of me. You connected me to my inner child and helped me to rebuild all the parts that were left broken and unseen. Thank you with all my heart and soul, James. I am forever in your debt.

Sonia, Tama and the I AM Healing Centre. Sonia, I walked into your centre many years ago and when I did, I was a broken girl; I had lost my way. Every Friday, you would, and still do, offer a one-and-a-half-hour meditation session that heals and transforms like no other. The first time I attended, I had never heard of sound bowls, high frequency music, nor did I sit in a circle with other human souls and have the confronting experience of staring directly into someone's eyes for three minutes. I had never done deep breathing nor had I ever taken my mind deep enough to travel through to other worlds and times. I found answers and guidance that I didn't even know existed through those times and places you took me to in deep meditation.

Although I didn't understand a lot of what was happening, the space you created allowed me to feel safe and allow my mind and body to let go switch of and actually see hear and listen like I have never done so before. From this experience, I soon chose to make your meditations my weekly, non-negotiable commitment to my healing into the woman I am today. Every meditation brought me closer to exactly where I am at today and I believe and know in my heart this is exactly where I'm meant to be. I can't thank you enough, Sonia, for providing such a magnificent place to come and heal and transform myself from dust to stone. It was here in your practice that I was exposed to many of the healers that I write about today and that have been a significant part of my healing journey. Thank you for being brave enough to show up as your authentic self and for gifting the world the opportunity to come to a place to heal. I am forever grateful for your vision, your heart, and your journey. I know there is no other place in this world like the I AM Healing Centre and I thank you every day that there is one.

Thank you, beautiful Belinda, for being your angelic, inspiring self. Your healings nurtured my soul and showed me a light that I forgot existed within me. Just being in your presence was a healing in itself. Thank you for connecting me to my past and to the goddesses that continue to exist and support me in this lifetime.

Emma, you have seen me in my early days, when I was weak, vulnerable and had lost my way. You only ever saw strength in me and were convinced that when I remembered who I was I would return her. For this, I will be forever grateful. It is the strength and courage that you bestow that helps me believe in myself. Thank you for being a pillar of strength when I needed it most.

Grounded Goddess, Vanessa, you are the ray of light, hope and all things true that this world needs. Your voice stands in its truth and grounds itself to the core of who you are and what you know. Your classes, events, readings, healings and teachings are all evidence of exactly this. You are a true leader and one that I proudly would stand by and follow through this life and many others. Whenever I leave you, I walk away feeling uplifted, inspired and confident in who I am and my place here on this Earth. Your energy is so uplifting, and you are an absolute joy to be around. I am so grateful for all your advice and guidance. You saw this book before I did and I'm so glad I can present it before you a few years later. Much gratitude and love to you always.

Dr Gerry Flynn. If it wasn't for you and your teachings, all those many years ago, I believe I would be a very different person today. Showing me how to connect to my resources within myself freed me of anxiety, panic attacks and living in fear. You changed my life and, in many ways, gave me one. I thank you, from the bottom of my heart. I will forever be grateful.

Dr Karen Coates. From a young girl to womanhood, you have shown me a side to health that has guided me into the right areas of my life. My health and wellbeing journey all began with you, and I thank you for not only healing me from the inside out, but for teaching me how to look at health holistically—as mind, body and soul as one. Thank you for taking my nature and character into account and guiding me to other specialists that would nurture those aspects within myself. You treated me as an individual and never as another number. You gave me a foundation to nourish and grow from and I am forever grateful to you.

Rick, what you and Selina have given me is more than I could ever repay you for. You offered me a job that provided an atmosphere many can only dream of working in. You were the boss of a lifetime and a person I can call a true friend. There was nothing I couldn't ask for and nothing you wouldn't do, for not only me, but for the people that work for you. Working for you was the break from the beauty industry I was so desperately craving. Thank you for hiring me; thank you for welcoming me into a world full of fun, happiness, parties and an extremely safe and trustworthy environment. I absolutely adored coming to work and loved the time in my life where I worked for the world's best boss. Rick, thank you for giving me the best wedding speech—one that, to this day, is remembered and treasured in my heart. Thank you for seeing me and for valuing the person I am. I certainly appreciate everything you and Selina have done for me and my family. I am forever grateful and always feel a part of the Ashmore crew.

Jess, I absolutely love being a part of your life. Thank you for opening your arms to me and supplying me with your abundantly joyful, full-of-laughter, happy, present world you live in. I admire most where your priorities lie in life, and I admire even more the willingness to ensure your loved ones' cups are always full and overflowing while attaining yours. This is such an important skill so many of us can acquire. Laughter really is the best medicine and you, my friend, give me plenty of it. Thank you, with all my heart. I love you.

Shellie, thank you for your beautiful supportive and encouraging heart. You light up my day every time I am in your presence. You are beautiful on the inside and out. You contain one of life's most valuable assets, Integrity. I love doing life with you and I love you.

Leah, you are the true definition of physical and emotional strength. I pity the person that doubts you in any way, as I believe there is nothing you couldn't achieve. There is so much about our human existence that we have been able to relate and share with one another. We have walked very similar paths here on this Earth and having your wisdom and hindsight has been a blessing and a support. So much of this book is for you.

Sandrine, you are the true meaning of warmth and heart. It is an absolute honour to be your Soul Sista. Thank you for seeing me, loving me and always being a friend that I can rely on. Having your beautiful soul live on this Earth is part of what makes this life a beautiful one to live in. Thank you for being a warmth in my life.

Sharon, I will forever be grateful for the beautiful person you are. Having you as a part of my everyday life has been a truly magical gift. You radiate everything that makes this human life beautiful, honest and true. Thank you for your sincerity and offering your heart when I needed it. You represent the true meaning of kindness and compassion. I adore and love you, Sharon. Thank you for being you.

Renae, from the moment I saw your beautiful face in the hospital during our first antenatal class, I knew I wanted to get to know you. You radiate an energy that I was completely drawn to. Twelve years later, two kids and a bag of memories, you have turned out to be more than just a friend—you are a part of my heart. I love you dearly and there is nothing I wouldn't do for you and your family. I believe we have lived a previous life together in which we were both warriors, fighting alongside one another, protecting one another and offering words of wisdom. So, there is no surprise that we have found ourselves doing exactly that together again in this life. Thank you for being on my side through emotional battles. Thank you for seeing me for who I am and for loving me as I am. I look up to you in so many ways. You are a jewel worth treasuring and I have kept you in a special place in my heart. I can't wait to see the world with you. I love you.

Marie, there is not a day that goes by that I don't thank the universe that you are in mine. You are the true meaning of mind-over-matter. Your positive and uplifting perspective and attitude towards life and everything you have had to face makes you a true leader and someone to aspire to be. You radiate happiness, joy and everything fun. Fate brought us together and it has been one of my life's biggest blessings to have you and your family openly welcome myself and my very own family into yours. I will be forever grateful to both you and John for offering me the safety, love, and unconditional support towards not only myself, but my family as well. I love you with all my heart, and I thank you for loving me, too. I know there is no such thing as the perfect human, but to me, you resemble exactly that. You will forever be imprinted in my heart.

Maddy, thank you for being exactly you. You are an incredible young woman with the integrity of a warrior. Thank you for being the amazing girl that you are. What you offer the world is priceless and worth bottling. Thank you for taking care of my two most prized possessions and for doing it with a fierce amount of sincerity. I loved that, inside of you, existed my very own brain; we think so much alike when it comes to ethics and life in general. You provided me what I call real help—unconditioned help. I will forever be grateful.

Kez, Mark and your whole family, what an honour it has been to be a part of your life. Thank you for welcoming myself and the boys into your hearts. You have provided us not only a lifelong friendship, but a place we can come to for unconditional love and support. Mark and Kez, you have managed to create a family that both Matt and I endeavour to create. Thank you for paving the most incredibly beautiful and wonderful path that we can only dream of following. You are incredible people and have created amazing children who have grown to be exceptional people and a pure reflection of their mum and dad. Your family is the perfect example of the meaning behind the name.

Thank you, Mark, for gifting me the ability to call you my brother. It warms my heart to know that I am worthy of such an honour. I want to acknowledge the wonderful man that you are to offer love, support generosity and kindness so freely, in spite of times in your own life when a name would portray you to be anything other than who you really are. They don't win. The truth of who we are will always prevail.

Kez, some people spend their whole life searching high and low to find beautiful, genuine real and honest souls like yourself. How extremely blessed I am to have found you in mine. You are one of the best friends I have; you are my soul sister. I thank you for the warmth you radiate from your heart directly into mine. Nothing about you is shallow; everything is deep, rich and to the core, and it's because of the extent of your depth, you have been so generous to provide me with, I have managed to heal into the person I am today. I will forever be grateful for you, Kez. I can't thank you enough for your support and encouragement.

You are a treasure worth cherishing for life and I plan to do exactly that. I love your heart and I love you.

Beck, the day I connected to my worth and chose to create healthy boundaries around it was the day I was gifted your magical friendship. You showed me a love that was soul deep. When I was happy, you felt joy; when I was sad, you felt sadness; when I was winning in life, you felt like you had won, too. You renewed a place in my heart that allowed me to open up and trust the female relationship again. It all begun with you, Beck. You are such a special woman and I love you so much. I can't thank you enough for seeing me for who I am on the inside. My love for you is soul-deep and it will never change. You are my soul family, and you are my family here on Earth. You brought me back to life and I will eternally be grateful to you, my sister, for this life and many more ahead.

Melissa Ambrosini. There have been many powerful, loving leaders in this world that many of us look up to and admire—people that make an everlasting impact on our lives here on Planet Earth. Princess Diana, Martin Luther King, Oprah Winfrey have all impacted and inspired my heart and time here on Earth, but it has been you, Melissa, that has made the most significant impact on not only my healing journey but my life as a whole. Your books were by my side through the toughest of times, offering me a voice of sincere truth and integrity. Your podcasts were, and still are, a place to find so many answers to my ever-growing questions. Everything you offer and all of who you are bring with it an abundance of unconditional support, love, hope and guidance.

Your heart was the love that brought me back to my core and made me believe in my truth. This world moves into more love and greatness because of Light Leaders like yourself. Thank you for helping me find my way back to me; your courageous and powerful voice made me believe in mine. There is no doubt that your work and all that you do for this universe will leave an ever-growing legacy for many future generations to follow. Thank you for igniting the beautiful shift this world needs. I will forever hold gratitude in my heart for you. I love you.

I would also like to thank your wonderful husband, Nick Broadhurst. Nick, your music lifted my soul and gave it a place to regenerate. In my dark moments, I would play Inner Love and Breath. While tears would stream down my face, I would close my eyes, sway to your music and allow my body to surrender the pian and lift it out of me. Your music has the power to heal and uplift and I thank you for providing such a gift to this world. Both you and Melissa have been such a positive influence on both my husband and I, and I know he personally wants to thank you too— our kids included. They are no stranger to The Melissa Ambrosini Show and the Nick Broadhurst Show; our whole family has flourished through both of your voices and the love you both place into this universe. Melissa and Nick, thank you from the bottom of our hearts. There will always be a place for you in my kingdom.

To the two sides of my heart, Ashton and Travis, thank you for choosing me to be your mum. I am so blessed to say I have two of the most beautiful boys that exist in this world. Having boys is an absolute blessing in itself. I promise to work hard every day to be the example, and not expect it from you. You owe me nothing. My wish for you is freedom. May you wake up every day knowing emotional freedom is your birthright. I accept you always, just as you are. I love you unconditionally and forever.

Travis

Travis, my beautiful unconditional loving soul. You are the light so many of us seek to find. A heart that generates a love that could melt the darkest of stone into the purest of water. Travis, you are a gift that continues to bring joy, love and laughter into not only my life, but everyone's life you grace. I thank you every day for showing me how you feel; for speaking up and for not being afraid to offer love and kindness in spite of the outcome. Feeling is your superpower, and I pray that you will always see the strength in that. It is an honour to be your mother, as it is even more so to learn from your empathy and willingness to see love in every situation. Promise me you will always give yourself as much love and joy that you so freely hand to others. You are worth all the love this lifetime has to offer. Thank you for being exactly who you want to be and nobody else. I will take much joy in spending the rest of my life watching you do just that. You are a rare and beautiful light. Travis, never stop shinning.

Ashton

Ashton, thank you for being "The Mighty Oak Tree". You bend and sway with the wind; your truth, your honesty and your individuality create an unshakable amount integrity within such a young person. Nothing and no one will blow you away from your truth as you stand firm in it. You have been this way from day one, and I admire the hell out of you. You are such an inspiration; I look up to you in complete awe knowing that I get to spend the rest of my life watching this beautiful oak tree flourish into even more of what it already is. It's my honour to be your mother. Thank you for showing me how to be something as strong and victorious as you are. You're capable of everything, Ashton, because everything is what you already are.

To my best friend in the universe, Matt. I believe more than anything that we signed up to do this life together. We suited-up in our armour, took one deep, soulful look into each other's eyes and said, "Right, let's go be humans together." Your perspective on life and everything in it is nothing short of inspiring. There isn't one day that I wake and don't feel complete admiration for you. You are an incredibly intelligent man who always sees every problem as an opportunity to learn, grow and adapt. For you, the glass is always half-full. Thank you for being the wonderful father you are to our boys, an incredible businessman, loving husband and a true friend. Thank you for supporting my independence and for loving the times when I believe in myself the most—the real Natalie. Thank you for not putting conditions on our love. The road at times has been rough, but rough is when we dig and that's what makes us stronger.

There is no way in this world that I would end this book without physically writing words of acknowledgement for what you have given me and the life you have provided me. What we do and what we have provided one another, on limited resources—and, in recent years, no resources apart from what we create internally and externally for one another—has been nothing short of monumental. I wanted to acknowledge all the item boxes we have provided ourselves our entire lifetime thus far. We are proof that you can do it on your own. Look at the life we have given one another; we are truly spectacular people; Matt. Nobody can take away what we have built and what we continue to build.

We nearly lost ourselves and had nowhere to turn but look at what we found when we thought we had nothing left to give. We found what we forgot we always had—each other, the kids and other lifelong souls that really do love us for who we are. Where we came from doesn't define us—what we do and the people we choose to be does. You are an incredible person, Matt. Never forget how much you offer the world we live in. I believe there is nothing that you couldn't master. I'd bet on you every day of the week and I'd go all in, knowing that I would never ever be disappointed.

I love you, Matt.

Quan Yin and Goddess Isis- my two spirit mothers that have guided me with their everlasting unconditional love, strenght and support. Thank you for finding your way to me in every lifetime.

And, finally, to the young girl inside of me, my inner child. It may have taken me 36 years, but I found us a place we can call home. A place where we are free to be all that we allow ourselves to be. A place where our heart, intention and the essence of who we are are so clear, it's never misconstrued, devalued, and taken advantage of. Instead, it's unconditionally loved, forever.

Natalie Falicz

www.thegirlbehindthecape.com

natalie@thegirlbehindthecape.com

Printed in Australia
AUHW011430180522
363806AU00050B/138